Enough

"Liberating yourself from controlling Jezebelic relationships."

By Robert & Dixie Summers

Enough

Published by
Summers Ministries
Columbus, Ohio

Enough
"Liberating yourself of controlling Jezebelic relationships" ©

Unless otherwise indicated, all scriptures used are from the King James Version of the Bible

Printed in the USA

ISBN
9798577710095

Dedication

This book is dedicated to our long-time friend Lorrie Robinson. Your friendship, kindness and support over the years has been tremendously valuable and appreciated. We think back on the many fond memories, whether during the tough times or the pleasant ones, we stuck together and grew through it all. Together, we've learned how to live free and enjoy God's blessings for our lives.

Lorrie, words alone cannot express the gratitude we have for you. Thank you so much for being there when we needed it the most. – Robert & Dixie

Table of Contents

Introduction

They live among us. They're everywhere and growing at an exponential rate. Hidden deep within families and societies for generations, they now manifest and are abusing the very lives of people that love them. Who and what are we referring to? We're talking about the controllers. These controllers can be your boss, a friend, your spouse, your parents, an adult child, and yes, even a governmental or religious leader.

Controlling others is a dominating spirit that sinks its fangs deep into the heart of its intended prey, releasing a series of vicious attacks that paralyze the mind, will, and emotions of the victim. When one has an appetite to control the life of another person, it is called abuse. The abusive behaviors can include (but are not limited to) physical or financial abuse, emotional and psychological abuse, which may involve an array of tactics such as intimidation, gaslighting, or aggression. These are the weapons of choice of a controller, as are verbal assaults designed to humiliate and breakdown an individual's self-worth. A controlling person is a very toxic, septic, and dysfunctional person. They harbor the insidious spirit known biblically as Jezebel.

The deep need to control others is a selfish and dysfunctional behavior designed to direct another person's life and serve the controller's purpose and desire. Both the demonic controlling entity and the person's controlling behavior will not let go as it seeks to enmesh their identity with that of the one they seek to control.

While controlling others may be a characteristic feature of the Narcissist, it does not mean that every controller has Narcissistic Personality Disorder (NPD). Today we have a plethora of people who use the label of 'narcissists' indiscriminately and often create more damage than good. Similarly, the absence of the controlling operation does not mean the person does not suffer from NPD. We must understand the stealth-like movement of a controller and the various mechanisms and tactics they use to keep their subjects in their grip.

However, control is a classic instrument used by the Spirit of Jezebel to 'slice and dice' its way through generations. And it is the primary operation used by the Narcissist's strategic campaign to dominate one's life and keep them in a constant state of confusion, helplessness, and despair. The need for one to control is a force so fierce that the controller is deceived by thinking they are normal. They are not normal, but instead, they are highly dysfunctional as their submission to this insidious spirit manifests through delusional ideologies, paranoid suspicions, manufactured stories, and constant drama.

The present-day surge and impact of Jezebel in society, government, families, and relationships have mostly gone unnoticed and remain in a place of darkness. To address this ancient spirit and the modern-day outbreak of controlling behavior is to go against the grain of a society laced with narcissistically minded people that possess a strong sense of entitlement and hatred of truth and righteousness. Yet, many find themselves at a crossroads where they can be silent no more. They have experienced a vast amount of pain and are looking for relief.

Compliance with the Jezebel spirit and the controlling behavior of its host's may yield short-term relief, but it is only kicking the can down the road. However, enabling or complying with a narcissistic controller is never the path to go.

The bible is very clear that we should not tolerate the spirit of Jezebel in our presence.

But I have this against you, that you tolerate that woman Jezebel .... Rev 2:20(a) (ESV)

Additionally, we are encouraged to expose the works of darkness.

Take no part in the unfruitful works of darkness, but instead expose them. Eph 5:11 (ESV)

Controlling others is a work of darkness, and if you're being controlled, it's time to break free from it. However, many are frustrated because while they know that being controlled is wrong and yields a tremendous amount of stress, strife, and anxiety in their life, they simply do not know how to break free.

But make no mistake, coming out of agreement with both the narcissistic controller and the witchcrafts of Jezebel will release persecution and a spirit of rage against you. Contending and challenging this spirit and its representatives will be met with resistance so fierce that you may wish you simply complied and surrendered to its demands for control. This battle is not for the faint in heart nor for those that want to stay stuck in self-pity or lay perpetually wounded on the battlefield of life. No, this is for the warriors that have had enough of the bondage of control.

Why we wrote this book

If you have been controlled or currently are in a controlling relationship, we wrote this book for you. It's designed to help those that have been blamed, shamed, attacked, and penalized for no apparent reason other than to become the controller's puppet that he or she can pin all their issues and toxic behaviors on. This book's primary focus is to help the reader better understand how control operates, where it comes from, the dangers of complying with it, how to respond to it, and ultimately get free.

Throughout this book, we may reference societal control. However, that is not the focus of this writing. Indeed, within the United States alone, we have a growing trend towards having a controlled society. Religious, governmental, and educational systems and the media and medical arenas all participate in creating and maintaining controlled environments. These systems tell you what to think and what you can and cannot do. They are the puppet masters that desire to control your life and demonize you if you resist these new "social norms." However, to discuss the various societal controls and the demonic principalities behind them would take up the entire book. Consider that topics like gun control or speech control alone would expand this book's size and scope.

Additionally, it is worth noting that this writing is not a religious one per se. It is a book written to help, encourage, equip, and heal people's hearts everywhere. It is designed to give you hope and realize that God has a beautiful future planned for you. However, it is a book that will provide Kingdom principles from the Word of God to assist you in your journey so you can live the abundant life intended for you.

This book is for those that want to take back their life. For the many people who didn't know any better, who thought that to be good enough and accepted, you needed to comply with the demands placed on you from other people. It is written for those that are tired of being doormats, whereby others walk all over them. It is also for the person who has been the punching bag for the abusive-controller to throw 'jabs' of shame and blame at. Finally, this book is for those who know that there is more to life than being enslaved by the needs of those that they have obsessively catered to. It is for those who want to discover their unique identity, to understand their purpose, and begin the journey of realizing their dreams and the pursuit of happiness. It's for those who know - enough is enough!

So, it's time to rise and say <u>ENOUGH!</u> Enough to the controllers that want to steal your time, treasure, and talent. Enough to the controlling Narcissistic-Jezebels that you've continually connected to in the hope that somehow you can fix them. You can't fix them, nor is it your responsibility to fix them. The only one that should control you is you. And if you are not in control of your life – then who is?

Remember, God did not create humanity to be controlled by anyone or anything. God gave us a free-will. Free-will is probably the greatest gift God has given humanity outside of our savior – the Lord Jesus. Moreover, God did not design mankind to control other humans, as He (God) doesn't control us.

Perhaps you have recently realized that you relinquished control of your life to the controller. More than likely, it's been decades that you've gone through this pain and torment, and now you're so worn down that you've normalized the dysfunction. Be aware that the road to regaining control over your life will not happen overnight. You must have a passionate desire to transform by renewing your mind and the way you think. You will need to unlearn the old habits and create new ones, ultimately developing healthy and positive behaviors in your life.

Finally, you will need emancipation from demonic spirits that have tormented you. If that's you and you accept this challenge, then start your journey by saying, "ENOUGH – I WILL NOT BE CONTROLLED ANYMORE."

Enjoy,

Robert and Dixie

Understanding Controlling Behavior

Controlling behavior is when one person expects, requires, or demands another person to satisfy their own needs at the other person's expense. Controlling behavior is the weapon of choice of a Narcissist – although not all controllers are narcissists. A controlling person is like a puppet master. The puppet master holds all the control. He decides every movement the puppet makes. The puppet has no say in the matter. The puppet is entirely under the power of the puppet master.

Definition of Control: *"The power to influence or direct people's behavior or course of events; to determine the behavior of or supervise the running of something or someone."*

Controlling behavior is typically found in individuals with a high level of anger and anxiety in their life. Rather than addressing their internal pain, fear, and wounds, they project their internal chaos into and onto the lives of other people. Controlling behavior is very selfish and self-seeking. It never considers the life, health, and wellness of other people. Control is a behavior that looks to dominate others.

A controlling person thinks their needs are more important than anyone else's, and they expect accommodation in everything. Their expectation of others and their perception of the world around them is a distortion from reality. They are only concerned with their feelings and their needs. Their view is one of entitlement and therefore expects you to be submissive to their demands. A controller will see any resistance or failure to comply as an attack on their authority over you.

Controlling people are self-centered and immature. Their behavior resembles little children that throw temper tantrums when they don't get their way. They pout, cry, kick, and scream until all the attention is on them. Controlling behavior lacks consideration, empathy, and respect and is the infiltration of others' personal space and resources. People look to control others because they have a deep fear of losing control. People who battle with controlling behaviors often fear being at the mercy of others. Their low self-esteem and lack of self-confidence make them feel helpless, vulnerable, and inferior to others. To compensate for this, they will establish superiority and dominance in their environment and relationships with others.

Controlling people are hazardous, and their behaviors are provoked by the insidious spirit known as Jezebel. Jezebel is the name associated with the characteristics of a controller. Jezebel is a seducing spirit that aims to bring you under her controlling power. This spirit will use many tactics (which we will discuss later) to seduce and control her prey. Witchcraft is at the core of Jezebel's network.

The Jezebel spirit uses the flesh to release witchcraft against the soul (mind, will, and emotions). The purpose of witchcraft is to weaken your will and ultimately control your life.

Controlling behaviors and Witchcraft

Being controlled by a person, organization, or network is VERY dangerous and can severely hinder your emotional and spiritual growth.

Control is a form of Witchcraft. "Witch-craft" (the craft of a witch) is designed to move you away from what God has shown you (i.e., your vision, your destiny, and your purpose) to what someone else is trying to show you and ultimately get you to do.

Witchcraft is a manifestation of the Flesh. It is the flesh's appetite (desire) to control you and dominate you through the use of intimidation and manipulation. Witchcraft is an attack against the mind, either directly or indirectly. Controlling people (many of which are Narcissistic-Jezebels) want to control their environment by mind manipulation. Tactics such as gaslighting, blame-shifting, and threats are deployed to get you to serve their perverted ideologies.

Walk in the Spirit, and ye shall not fulfil the lust of the flesh.
Galatians 5:16

You can either walk in the Flesh or walk in the Spirit, but you cannot walk in both simultaneously. Walking is the Spirit means you conduct, regulate, navigate, and govern your life based on the Word of God. Believers are called to walk in the Spirit, and they will NOT fulfill the flesh's lust. The Flesh has passion or desire. The Flesh is the carnal mindset of the old sin nature and is referred to in the bible as the 'old man.' Paul talks explicitly about Witchcraft in the book of Galatians. He warns us of its operation and effects.

O foolish Galatians, who hath bewitched you, that ye should
not obey the truth, before whose eyes Jesus Christ hath been
evidently set forth, crucified among you? This only would I learn
of you, Received ye the Spirit by the works of the law, or by the
hearing of faith? Are ye so foolish? having begun in the Spirit,
are ye now made perfect by the flesh? – Gal 3:1-4

Notice the words bewitched, spirit, and flesh. The word BEWITCHED is the Greek word "baskaubaino," which is used for a blinding effect of the evil eye and has an occult reference, but it has nothing to do with sorcery. Instead, it means to be charmed, seduced, or bound by someone or something in your thoughts and emotions, to speak ill of one, to slander or criticize someone.

Paul ties witchcraft to the flesh here and in the book of Galatians

The acts of the flesh are obvious: sexual immorality, impurity and debauchery; idolatry and <u>witchcraft</u>; hatred, discord, jealousy, fits of rage, selfish ambition, dissensions, factions and envy; drunkenness, orgies, and the like. I warn you, as I did before, that those who live like this will not inherit the kingdom of God - Galatians 5:20

Witchcraft is the Greek word "Pharmakeia," meaning to be poisoned, infected, made toxic, septic, diseased, and disillusioned. Today we would call this a Mind-altering drug.

Control is a manipulative toxin that gets you to change (alter) your mind unwillingly or through the use of fear and drama. CONTROL is a feature of WITCHCRAFT.

Witchcraft will do whatever it takes to control the environment around it. The manipulation of energy causes psychic attacks through negative vibration projected at a person or place, which will create disturbances in mind, emotions, and a person's physical body. You could see this negative energy as a spirit, an entity, a being, a thought form where harm is intended for a person or place.

16

"Witchcraft is the fleshes craving to control and dominate a person, specifically through the use of intimidation and manipulation."

Controllers utilize psychic attacks (i.e., witchcraft) to transfer dark and negative energies to their targets. At times this can occur without a person meaning to do so. For example, they may have had a negative thought that triggered a negative emotion such as jealousy, anger, or rage. The flip side is that some people intentionally create harm and damage by using control and manipulation to punish someone.

The origin of controllers

The desire to control is similar to witchcraft because it stands in total contradiction to God's nature. He gave the gift of free will to all humanity, and He refuses to violate that gift. He will encourage us, draw us and attempt to lead us, but He always leaves it up to us to choose His way:

I call heaven and earth to record this day against you, that I have set before you life and death, blessing and cursing: therefore choose life, that both thou and thy seed may live - Deuteronomy 30:19

Controlling people are responsible for their actions. They chose to control. While they will typically look to blame others for their actions, they must be exposed for their actions and be made accountable.

Controllers can learn it through someone that did it to them. Typically, this is found within the family of origin, perhaps a Narcissistic father or Jezebelic-Controlling mother. For instance, a man might duplicate the behavior of his Narcissistic-Controlling father. If he had an abusive father (physical, drugs, alcohol, perversion, womanizer, etc.), the son (as a young child) may have wanted this dysfunctional behavior to stop to receive the affirmation, validation, and love he so desperately needed from his father. As the son transitions into an adult, he may end up controlling others in an attempt to get the attention he needed as a child from his father. Additionally, a young male may develop a controlling personality out of hurt and resentment towards his mother's unwillingness to protect him when he was a young child.

Females with a dominating (Jezebelic) mother and a passive (Ahab-type) father may follow the example exhibited before her and become very controlling herself. Some women abused by the men in their lives (i.e., fathers, brothers, past relationships, etc.) will release Jezebel's vengeance attempting to get back at men because they feel they have been victimized. Many victims retaliate by controlling others. Control provides them with a sense of false justice as they look to "even the score" in life.

Women not protected by healthy fathers or those with no father-daughter relationship can become emotionally wounded at a young age. As they go through life, they may experience additional trauma (hurt) at the hands of controlling men. In an attempt to anesthetize their wounded emotions, they can become exactly like that which they despise, a controller. Rather than being controlled - they learn to control. They control to protect themselves from the cruelty of Narcissistic-Controlling men. Their woundedness is obvious, and they frequently become defensive, angry, bitter, rude, vindictive, and callous in their emotional attachment themselves.

Controllers, whether male or female, are highly skilled at seduction, criticism, and blaming. Through years of seeking out their prey, they become master manipulators and powerful intimidators who wreak havoc in others' lives. All of this is part of the Jezebel network features.

Furthermore, some grew up in homes where the family of origin or caretakers did not have any boundaries. The family was dysfunctional and out of control. In cases like this, a child can feel unprotected. Later on, in life, they may control others to provide a sense of safety and security.

People become controllers if they think they lack control over any part of their own life. The feeling of being out of control can motivate a person to regain control. While there's nothing wrong with regaining or establishing control over one's own life, the problem arises when the control extends into areas that one does not have ownership over.

A person may develop a controlling personality if they have been abandoned by others, specifically their family of origin. A son abandoned at a young age by his father may grow up and look to control his mother because deep in his subconscious mind, he fears losing his mother. A wife who fears that her husband may cheat on her might become very controlling. A single mother abandoned by her male companion might have a phobia of losing her teenaged son to 'another woman,' and control him by imposing extraordinary restrictions on him.

Control originating from Shame

In many cases, a controller may have been exposed to past traumatic experiences. Emotional, psychological, and physical abuse from the family of origin or a close 'friend of the family' may have developed into demonic strongholds of rejection. Shame is closely aligned with rejection and can be highly painful to the one suffering from it. While controllers certainly act like megalomaniacs, they are very fragile at their core. Controllers come from shame-based systems. These systems can be cultural, ancestral, religious, or societal based. Shame is learned. We are not born ashamed. Places, where shame is learned are:

1. Family of origin
2. Trauma
3. Religion
4. School
5. Society (race, sex, class, etc.)

Indications that shame exists can be when a person feels the need to control others. Passive-aggressive and abusive behaviors, power struggles (as to who is right and who is wrong), and always needing to be number one are signs of shame. Shame is learned through painful experiences in life, specifically in childhood, with one's family of origin.

Shame-based families lack boundaries. The lack of boundaries and limits is an unhealthy trait that's passed on for generations. When healthy boundaries are not present, it sets the stage for issues to arise in power and control. That is due to the lack of understanding where one's life stops, and another person's life begins. Controllers will always violate others' rights, mainly since someone most likely violated their rights by being abused as a child, either physically, emotionally, or sexually.

Adults shamed as children are afraid of being vulnerable and fear exposure of self. They also feel as if they are inferior to others. They don't believe they make mistakes; instead, deep in their core, they think they are a mistake. To compensate for this pain, they control and abuse other people. Adults shamed as children may appear grandiose and self-centered. They frequently feel defensive even when minor negative feedback is given.

Adults shamed as children consistently blame others before they can be reprimanded for their actions. They suffer from debilitating feelings of anger and judgment towards others. Shame-based controllers feel as though they must get what they want to be happy. They believe that other people want (or should want) the same things that they do. Shame creates a foundation for the development of a narcissistic controller.

The role of life commandments and control

Each of us has life commandments that govern our life in various ways. A life command is a standard way that we conduct our lives daily. Life commandments are learned at a very young age, usually from zero through 12 years. They are taught by the people closest to us that we give authority to. Examples would be parents, close relatives, schoolteachers, and church leaders.

Life commandments can be positive or negative. Experiences, training, and relationships have a tremendous impact on developing these commandments, ultimately becoming our code of conduct. Life commandments exist deep in the subconscious mind and direct behaviors – both healthy and unhealthy. Controlling others is toxic behavior that comes from negative life commandments.

Negative life commandments can become a significant factor that leads to a controlling personality. If a person learned that they are not in control of their life or feel helpless and powerless, they will most likely become dysfunctional in choices and control others to compensate for their internal struggle. If they have a subconscious paradigm and a life command that consistently says, *"I am insignificant"* or *"I am a failure"* or perhaps *"I am inadequate,"* this could cause anxiety and lead them to control and manipulate others.

Control and its connective features of manipulation, intimidation, and anger create a pseudo personality in the controller's life. A false character (false self) is designed to counter the growing anxiety and to self-medicate the pain of feeling inferior and insecure. Controlling others helps the controller maintain their denial of problems and keep the true self safe and hidden.

An unstable life

Controllers are extremely unstable in their behavior and life in general. Many of them are double-minded.

But let him ask in faith, with no doubting, for he who doubts is like a wave of the sea driven and tossed by the wind. For let not that man suppose that he will receive anything from the Lord; he is a double-minded man, unstable in all his ways. James 1:6-8 (NKJV)

The phrase (double-minded) is translated as "two-minds" and originates from the Greek word meaning 'split soul' or 'split mind.'

Schizo = Split / Phren = Mind or Schizophrenia.

Controllers have intense and unstable emotions and are incredibly moody. They are shapeshifters that closely resemble the Jekyll-Hyde operation, whereby they move in and out of passive and aggressive emotions quite quickly. Controllers may have Schizophrenia or Borderline Personality Disorder.

Controllers act on impulse without considering the consequences of their actions. Due to their high level of pride and lack of respect towards others, controllers periodically find themselves in deep trouble with their employer, the legal system (the law) and may even be incarcerated. Interestingly controllers are often prone to accidents or experiencing dramatic events in their life.

They are often highly theatrical in projecting their life to others. They will share their life with others and paint a picture that everything in their life is falling apart, and somehow you are the blame for it, or at the very least partly responsible. Controllers will embrace their dramatic life and use it as a way to gather sympathy or pity. Many times, this becomes the gateway to initiating or cultivating a dysfunctional relationship with others.

Individuals that have controlling behavior need deliverance and healing. Additionally, life and relationship coaching will help them identify unhealthy behavior and understand why they behave the way they do. Once identified, the individual can begin the journey of discovering the real self, learn how to enjoy wholesome relationships, and achieve their full potential in life.

Types of Control

Several categories need to be looked at when it comes to controlling people. Lovers, spouses, close friends, parents, in-laws, siblings, adult children, religious leaders, and organizations are some of the more prevalent areas. Many of these areas either go unnoticed, or we can be in denial that the control exists. Denial is an accommodating defense. There are many reasons why one may be in denial, including avoidance of physical or emotional pain, trauma bonding, or the fear of engaging in conflict with the controller. Often, it's is due to embarrassment and shame. Embarrassment, in many cases, is a secondary emotion derived from shame.

People who find themselves participating in controlling relationships may continue in that toxic relationship out of their sense of embarrassment and shame. A mindset exists that the relationship must be perfect, and as such, one will not expose the dysfunction. Although the stress of being controlled is present, the need to impress others, and the addiction to earning approval and acceptance will often bring one to self-delusion and denial. Controllers will exploit any vulnerability that may exist in their targeted prey. Let's explore some of the areas of control.

Relationship Control (Romantic-Lovers)

This is the area where most people experience the pain and frustration of being controlled. Controlling relationships are toxic and extremely dangerous. Unfortunately, it's not always easy to recognize you're being controlled until your deep into the relationship, and the damage has gone deep down to several levels. The reason it's not easy is not due to 'red flags' or danger signs not posted - because they were. You most likely ignored them because you were in the first stage of the gaslighting protocol of the Narcissistic Controller called the "Honeymoon stage."

Gaslighting is a form of psychological abuse used by narcissistic controllers to impart an extreme sense of anxiety and confusion in their victims to the point where they no longer trust memory, perception, or personal judgment. The techniques utilized are similar to those used by the military and intelligence personnel to interrogate and torture opposing forces. A controller uses gaslighting to terrorize its target emotionally.

The "Honeymoon Stage" of gaslighting is where the narcissistic controller (i.e., Jezebel) puts on his or her best face. More realistically, we could call it a false face. It's false because what is on display is designed to lure you into becoming emotionally entangled with a performance that does not represent the real person. The honeymoon stage will make you feel as though you are the only person in the world and that you are the only person that understands the controller. The controller initially sets you by getting you emotionally attached to their illusion that you are the person they need and can turn to. Of course, this is all smoke and mirrors to get you to take the bait so they can set the hook into your life.

Included in this stage is "love-bombing."

Love bombing is an attempt to use attention and affection to influence another person. It is a tool of manipulation that resembles infatuation with a particular person. Love bombs are a type of false love. A bombardment of false-love by a person exists to conceal the real intention – establish control. The controller uses love-bombing to make you feel special and to gain a level of trust. It's a warm feeling, especially for individuals starving for acceptance, attention, and affection. Love bombing can manifest in many ways; however, they're recognizable through some of the following actions:

- Excessive phone calls, text messages, and emails
- Excessive desire to contact you (physically or virtually) throughout the day
- Buying you expensive gifts
- Spending excessive time with you to make you feel #1
- Suffocating you with admiration and praise
- Flattering you, adoring you, and telling you how beautiful, precious and unique you are
- Telling you that they cannot live without you or that you are their 'soul-mate.'

While the list can go on and on, what's important to understand here is that none of these things in and of themselves are necessarily wrong. They're just not genuine and real. When originating from the heart of a wounded, angry, raged narcissist, they are insidious and nothing more than a well-executed strategy against you to lure you into the web of destruction.

Indeed, there is a sense of euphoria when one connects with a person that appears interested, kind, and caring. Perhaps they share some common interests such as nature, art, or sports. Or they come across as a person that has it all together. They're successful in their careers, have a charismatic personality, and share the same faith as you. Could it get any better than this? Is it too good to be true? But be aware, this is the honeymoon stage where the narcissistic controller looks to sweep you off your feet.

Once the bond of trust is built with the controller, the "devaluation" operation begins. This campaign is composed of various mind games. Criticism, blame, name-calling, accusation, manipulation, control, and emotionally abusive behavior are just a few examples. This can go on for years and intensify the longer you're in a relationship with a control freak. In some cases, it can be a lifelong ball and chain designed to weigh you down with depression, hopelessness, and despair.

Controlling relationships are not unique to romantic relationships only.

Relationship Control in Parents

Parents' relationships with their now-grown children should be healthy. They should be encompassed by love and have mutual respect for personal boundaries that are established. It is vital for parents and now grown adult children to recognize that everyone has their separate identity in life. When this is not recognized and respected, abuse is inevitable.

Parents that control their now-adult children are wounded individuals that most likely did not get the love, affirmation, validation, and protection they needed when they were young themselves. Unfortunately, their dysfunction will have a generational effect as they look to aestheticize their internal pain by controlling their sons and daughters.

Controlling parents are abusive parents that demand to be the center of attention in the adult child's world. They are unwilling to cut the parental bond with their child. Both parents may control the adult child or only one parent. If it's only one parent, perhaps the mother, the father (if present) will usually be a passive-Ahab type of individual that does not want to 'rock the boat 'within his marriage or, worse yet, experience the wrath of his Narcissistic-Jezebelian wife.

Exploring the inter-workings of controlling parents could easily be a book by itself. Here, we will discover some of the manifestations of controlling parents.

Controlling mothers (with their sons)

Mothers control their sons differently than their daughters. For example, a mother who experienced trauma in childhood herself, especially at her father's hands, can become overly controlling of her adult son. Further, suppose the mother experienced a bad marriage where the husband was not emotionally connected. In that case, the mother may look to her son to fulfill her emotional void and crave attention, validation, support, and protection. The mother herself most likely had 'daddy' bonding issues and will look to emotionally marry her 'daddy figure.' In time, she will flip that toxic emotion to the son once she sees the husband cannot comply with her perverted needs. The mother will then look to the son as a replacement for the emotionally depleted husband.

Controlling mothers often praise their sons to others and sport them like trophies. Her deep insecurities and the insatiable need to have a male submit to her is exceptionally prevalent. Controlling mothers often emasculate their sons, never permitting them to grow and develop as independent males. Mothers that continue to care for their grown sons well into their twenties, thirties and beyond, create friction in the home. Many of these males may grow up angry at women or engage in perversive sexual activities.

The mother may become entangled with the son and expect the son to meet the mother's emotional needs. Many times this is referred to as emotional incest. In extreme control cases, the mother may physically seduce her son by flirting, touching, and caressing the son. This is designed to deepen the toxic soul-tie with the son by injecting a tremendous amount of guilt and shame into the son. The son's feeling of guilt and shame will be used against him as he grows and attempts to emancipate himself from his mother. As the son matures intellectually, physically, and ages chronologically, his emotions are arrested at the point of the soul-tie (trauma) with the mother. He is never able to grow emotionally outside of his mother's control. His confidence, self-respect, and identity is tied to his mother's approval.

Signs of independence from the son will be met with vengeance, drama, or manipulation from the mother as she does not want her son to leave her emotionally. Controllers do not want their sons to have any healthy relationship with women. They'll sabotage relationships, marriages, and independent dreams. Whether girlfriends or a wife, women will be seen as the enemy and attacked consistently, howbeit in a covert manner. Wives married to men that have experienced Maternal Narcissistic Abuse will typically experience the brunt of the pain released by the now-adult son. While internally, the son is angry at his controlling mother, he has been groomed for loyalty and devotion. He has served in his mother's Jezebelic bedchamber. His anger will only provoke abuse against himself through addictions (i.e., alcohol, drugs, porn, career) or abuse towards his spouse, typically manifesting as emotional disconnection.

Remember controlling mothers are deeply wounded themselves. More than likely, they suffered at the hands of their parents, specifically the fathers. Mothers that experienced rejection, abandonment, or abuse by the father may compensate by developing this unhealthy bond with her son.

Controlling mothers (with their daughters)

A controlling mother wants things to go her way all the time. She will often use yelling, blaming, guilt, drama, and manipulative words to get her way. Controlling mothers are usually angry and bitter women. They're miserable, unhappy, and have a sense of insignificance deeply embedded in their core. As such, they may manifest extreme abuse towards their daughter(s). Although abuse can be directed at any of the daughters within the family of origin, it is common for the oldest daughter to experience the brunt of the other's dysfunction. While all daughters are affected, the oldest (1st born) daughter is targeted most by the mother's aggressive-overt behaviors. While the Narcissistic-Jezebelian mother will ultimately control all the daughters, the manifestations are different.

Mothers control their daughters using a variety of tactics. One of them is by projecting their life onto and into their daughter. When a mother has lived her life in a less than fulfilling manner, she feels that she was short-changed and is full of regret and hopelessness. A daughter could be her escape from the pain. She will turn her daughter into a 'Barbie Doll' type of figure, whereby she lives out her fantasies throughout her daughter's life. This is highly toxic and dangerous for the daughter as it prevents her from personal emotional growth and development in addition to establishing her own identity. Many times, the daughter will feel suffocated and trapped by her mother's needs.

Additionally, a mother may control her daughter because she feels threatened by her daughter's sexuality and appearance. As the mother ages and perhaps her sexuality declines while the daughter's peaks, she may become jealous and resentful. This occurs many times when the father gives attention to the daughter and not the wife. Fathers that are complimentary towards their daughters only can cause these wives to resent the daughter. While fathers should complement their daughters, they must maintain a balance and not connect to the daughters in an unhealthy manner. That said, narcissistic mothers can control daughters to keep them from their fathers or men in general.

Women who have experienced abuse from men in their lives, either their father, lover, or husband, may retaliate against daughters through the malicious mother syndrome. Malicious mother syndrome (aka Malicious Parent Syndrome) is where (in this case) the mother attempts to punish the divorcing husband (father) through alienating their children (daughter) from the other parent. Mothers that demonize fathers to their daughters create an illusion that they are perfect and victims of the father's abuse. An example would be a mother telling her daughter (child) they could not afford to live in a decent neighborhood because their father had wasted all their money on other women. This is abusive and can develop a view in the daughter's mind that her mother was abused and victimized, having no chance to make it in life. While there is no denying that the mother experienced abuse and hardship, it is unhealthy to invoke self-pity to generate support for one's emotional wounds and instability. Mothers may turn to young daughters as a sounding board to express their anger, pain, or sadness.

Mother wounds are areas where controlling behavior and spirits can profoundly affect the daughter's personal growth and development. Mother wounds are established at a young age and connect to the daughter via the hypnotic suggestion, planting a seed of thought that suggest "I was responsible for my mother's pain," and "I can make my mother happy if I'm a good daughter."

The truth is that you weren't and still aren't responsible for your mother's pain – she is. You also can't make our mothers happy. Happiness is a decision, and she must decide for herself to be happy. Unfortunately, as a young daughter, you were not consciously aware of this, and subconsciously you may still believe that you are the reason for your mother's torment.

Controlling mothers can be vastly critical of their daughter. A critical mother is never pleased; no matter what you do or how good you are, she will always find something to criticize. Sometimes the mother is fearful of not wanting the daughter to make the same mistakes as she did. As such, everything the daughter does is regarded as a failure. The daughter can never be good enough. She can always do better. Perfection is the only thing that will yield any type of validation and affirmation. When the daughter does fail, the controlling mother will capitalize on the opportunity to 'swoop in' and make things better, thus forging a dependency on the mother.

Jealousy is another tactic used by controlling mothers. A mother may grieve at their unfulfilled dreams, unrealized talent, and unvalidated lives, looking at her daughter with envy due to the opportunities provided to the daughter. A mother may also become extremely envious as the daughter goes through puberty and begins to develop physiologically. Skin tone, color, hair, eye color, breasts, hips, lips, and legs may be looked at with an envious eye. The jealousy may be partly associated with the fact that her daughter is growing into a woman, which reminds her narcissistically controlling mother that she's getting older.

Narcissistic mothers will see their blossoming daughters as threats to their own identity and develop an insidious hatred towards them. Controlling mothers demean, ridicule, criticize and undermine their daughters. As the daughter grows up, the mother, who should nurture and permit the daughter to have an independent life, becomes threatened and jealous of the daughter's growing independence and ultimate autonomy. A mother's jealousy is often manifested as emotional withdrawal, criticism, and anger. When mothers get jealous of their daughters, it's usually best for their daughters to create boundaries and some distance between their mother and themselves. Furthermore, adult daughters who have children of their own need to protect their children from the controlling mother's unhealthy behaviors. Unprotected children will be targets of control themselves as the jealous mother continues her campaign to ultimately destroy the family and perpetuate the toxic behavior for generations to come.

Unhealthy, wounded, and controlling mothers can (at times) display extreme hatred and malicious behavior towards their daughters. These behaviors are toxic and insidious. Fighting, aggressive behavior, contention, cussing out, physical beatings, gossip, slander, explosive trauma and drama, rage, alienation, and sexual exploitation are ways controlling mothers bring damage to their daughters.

Controlling mothers may be more obscure in their behavior. Psychological manipulation, mind tricks, guilt trips, self-pity, and gaslighting are some of the applications used to control. On the surface, the mother may appear to be humble and self-sacrificing. Everything she does is for the benefit of her daughter. However, much of this is a smokescreen to cover-up from being seen as a less than perfect mother.

In short, a controlling mother can crush the daughter's emotional development and self-awareness. The demands and pressures placed on the daughter is seen in much of the anxiety, depression, and PTSD seen in women today.

Some signs that your mother could be controlling are:

- She requires you to act like her best friend (daughters)
- She acts as if you are her husband (sons)
- She demands your attention
- She is highly dependent on you
- She dictates what you will do
- She demands you carry out her commands
- She doesn't consider your feelings
- She's highly dramatic and sensationalizes any movement that goes against her wishes
- She cries, pouts, invokes depression and sickness upon herself to manipulate you to do her bidding
- She's overly protective and worries about you constantly
- She scrutinizes everything. Your social life, friends, foods you eat, and appearance
- She violates your privacy and disrespects your boundaries
- She's overly critical of you
- She uses guilt to control and manipulate you
- She uses power (money and position) to control, manipulate and dominate you
- She gives you the silent treatment
- She makes you feel responsible for her happiness

Controlling Spouses

Is my spouse a narcissist or a controller? That is a common question we get from our coaching clients. The answer depends on the further investigation of behaviors, emotions, thoughts, and background. However, whether a narcissist or a controller, both are damaging to any relationship and individual. Spousal control is relationship control on steroids. That is due to marriage bonds both from a religious, legal perspective, cultural and societal perspective. Whereas a 'lover' may divest from the relationship at the early signs of control, it's not that easy for a spouse, especially if children are in the equation.

Spousal control is where one person in the marriage wants to control the where, who, what, and why. Controlling spouses act out of a sense of emotional instability and vulnerability. They usually come from a shame-based platform derived from the family of origin. Controlling spouses are insecure individuals that lack confidence in who they are. They have a low self-image and were deeply rejected as children. As such, their only means of self-validation is to exercise control and domination over another person. Controllers use a wide range of weaponry to control and dominate their spouses. The objective of the narcissistic controller is to inflict pain on their spouse. That is no laughing matter and must be taken seriously. If you are being controlled, you must act now! Sweeping controlling characteristics and behavior under the rug or kicking them down the road only intensified the controller's septic nature and positions one for years of emotional stress, anxiety, fear, and torment.

Some of the signs and behaviors to recognize your spouse is controlling you are:

Fear and intimidation

If you are afraid about speaking up or giving your opinion to your spouse, or if and when you do, you are attacked, criticize, and ridiculed, then you are being controlled. Controllers love to intimidate and will threaten you in a variety of ways ranging from "I'll leave you, and no one will want you" or "If you do that again, you'll regret it."

Criticism

Controlling spouses are notorious for intense criticism targeted at their partner. Constant criticism and sarcastic statements regarding the way you look, dress, how you wear your hair, walk, talk, sit, stand, your friends, the food you eat, your job, what you do with your free time, how and what you think, your personal views and even your performance in the bedroom. These criticisms might start small, but they will grow exponentially over time. Any defense to the criticism will be met with a volley of anger and retaliation designed to bring you to a place of submission.

Guilt, Shame, and Blame

Controlling spouses are skilled at blaming you and making everything your fault. Rather than invest in a healthy dialog to understand their partner's feelings, they will unload a cesspool of guilt and blame upon you. The goal is to instill in you a sense of devaluation, worthlessness, and shame. While projected guilt will have you consistently thinking you did something wrong, shame will have you thinking that you are something wrong. You will feel as though you've done something wrong when, in fact, you've done nothing wrong.

Additionally, you will find yourself apologizing for wrongs you've never committed or seeking forgiveness from your spouse for not complying with their wishes. Controlling spouses rarely repent and express no feelings of remorse for their behavior or the hurts they inflict. Controllers demand compliance with their expectations on how you should act. Spouses that control will consistently bring up past failures, mistakes, errors, situations, and conversations. They never let you move forward. They control you by keeping you in bondage to your past, reminding you of behaviors that invoke spirits of shame, guilt, and condemnation.

Controlling spouses will blame someone for virtually everything that goes wrong and has gone wrong in their life. After the husband is finished blaming his mommy, he will pick up where he left off - blaming his wife. Once the wife is finished blaming her daddy, she will attack the husband. Controlling spouses will blame you for their failure and wrong decisions. They never look at themselves and what they did to contribute to their issues and toxic lifestyle, but instead, they blame you. All marital problems are blamed on the other spouse. You become the spousal scapegoat. Blame statements such as "If you didn't make me so angry all the time, I wouldn't explode at you" or "I would have never committed adultery, but you made me feel so unappreciated" are samples of what might be said.

Never accept the blame from a controlling narcissistic spouse. God's word says you are blameless:

Yet now he has reconciled you to himself through the death of Christ in his physical body. As a result, he has brought you into his own presence, and you are holy and blameless as you stand before him without a single fault. - Col 1:22 (NLT)

Controlling siblings

Siblings are a blessing. However, there are times where they cross personal boundaries, invade our space, and look to control a specific brother or a sister or all siblings. Problems often start right after the birth of the second child. Firstborn children can become the golden child and can be highly susceptible to narcissistic characteristics and behaviors. They can become control freaks that go to extraordinary measures to reign king of the hill. They will often team up with a controlling Jezebel mother to gain ranking within her bedchamber.

Children born after the firstborn can be jealous of the firstborn. That can be due to a variety of reasons. Regardless, the sibling will attempt to gain favor with the parents by demonizing the 1st born. They will cause division and strife between other siblings through manufactured lies and events.

The medieval proverb "blood is thicker than water" has been used by many controlling siblings and family members far too often to tolerate and accept vile, toxic, and dysfunctional controlling behaviors. Controlling siblings will turn other family members against you. They jockey for position and look for favoritism from parents, aunts, and uncles. Older sisters may seek to 'mother' the rest of the tribe. Controlling brothers may take on the 'alpha-dog' role and strive to be served by all others.

Controlling siblings do what they want to do, when they want to do it, how they want to do it. It's all about what they want. They decide where the family will spend the holidays, the food that will be served, and who will be invited.

Controlling siblings manipulate you into helping them out. You're always helping them move, babysit their kids, bailing them out of some financial or legal situation, you spend countless hours listening to their drama about whatever is affecting them that day. When it comes to an elderly parent and tending to their needs, they manipulate and control you to take care of most caregiving tasks.

All this leaves you exhausted, frustrated, and miserable. Interestingly enough, when you need help, they're never there for you. Instead, they will condemn you and place much guilt on you.

Controlling siblings are rival siblings. Many times, they are narcissistic, displaying callous, unsympathetic attitudes. The controlling sibling views others as opponents in a game of domination and control. The relationship among siblings can become highly competitive, at least with the controllers, and is infused with animosity, jealousy, and at times fighting. A Narcissistic-controlling sibling will often keep the score in life. They will keep a mental log of what you received in life versus them. Whether from your parents, friends, or personal achievement, the controller will view this as an insult to their entitled view of self.

Because of the controlling sibling's manipulative nature, they have most likely been very successful at disguising their toxic behavior, thus keeping it hidden from their parents. Many have taken on the "Golden-Child" or "I'm so mistreated" label and can do no wrong in mommy's or daddy's eye. Parents, especially as they get older, will usually dispute or discard any other children's attempts to expose the controlling sibling's behavior. Often, the parents will enable the narcissistic sibling and tell the other children "be nice to your brother or sister" and demonize you for your frustration and concern. At times this may require you to go no contact with the sibling or break away perhaps temporarily from the entire family system due to its enabling nature.

A controlling sibling will manipulate aged parents, especially in the area of finances. They will seek payments, bailouts, loans, and will even steal money from parents. When parents die, the controlling sibling will take care of all the arrangements and control all the financial affairs. They will control trusts, estate wills, who gets the money, the house, or other assets. However, they will not pay any of the bills or liabilities. Instead, they will place that burden on other family members.

Controlling Adult Children

Controlling adult children are dangerous and can be narcissistic adults. Many parents have difficulty acknowledging that their now-adult son or daughter is a narcissistic abuser or a control freak. To the parent, they see their child as their "baby," and while there is undoubtedly affection and love towards their children, they must realize that they are independent of them and need to be treated with respect and honor.

It can be a tremendous shock to parents that their little boy or girl has grown into a full-blown narcissistic abuser that has turned totally against them and craves to control, manipulate, intimidate and dominate your life. While these are your children, they are also toxic, sceptic, and insidious individuals that are hell-bent on making you miserable in life.

Controlling adult children will manifest in diverse ways, and there are some tactics used by male adult children that are unique to them as opposed to the operations of a female adult child. However, overall the intention is the same – punish the parents.

Narcissistic-controlling adult children place enormous demands on their parents to do what they want. They are emotionally glued to some trauma that occurred in their life. Their anger and rage are designed to control and intimidate their now aged parents. They plow through and disregard every boundary you have. To the controlling adult child, you are their problem. Every issue, horrible decision, economic shortfall, poor relationship, and lack they've experienced in life is your fault.

They will wear you down with guilt and blame. Guilt and blame are always at the center of the strategic, manipulative campaign against you. They will blackmail you by withholding your grandchildren from you. They will try to intimidate you by yelling, screaming, and using profanity, getting right up in your face to deposit seeds of fear and torment in your life.

Controlling adult children want to blame and shame you and work hard to get you into a battle. They want to fight, and they want you to trigger and "go off the deep end." Their strategy is to work you up into a frenzy and wear you down so much that you blow up and engage in the fight. That is necessary for them because they need to bring you down to their horrible level of self-worth to feel better about themselves by devaluing you.

Controlling adult children always want more and will beat you into submission if you do not do what they want you to do. Of course, every time you give them what they want, they will ultimately demand something else. Controlling adult children are like leeches. They can never let you go. They want to control you, your marriage, and your life. They do not want you to disconnect from them. They want more; they want everything you have.

The horseleech hath two daughters, crying, Give, give. There are three things that are never satisfied, yea, four things say not, It is enough - Proverbs 30:15

As parents to these controlling adult sons and daughters, you cannot give them what they want. The moment you do, they will demand something else. They will guilt you and shame you for every offense they accuse you of committing against them when they were little kids. Do not accept this blame and guilt from your controlling narcissistic adult children.

Parents are to be honored, not abused.

Children obey your parents in the Lord: for this is right. Honor thy father and mother; (which is the first commandment with promise;) That it may be well with thee, and thou mayest live long on the earth. Ephesians 6:1-3

No one deserves to be controlled and abused, especially elderly parents. Even if you were not the perfect parent, you gave your children what you thought was right at the time. There's no class you took in high school or college that could have prepared you for the intricacies of healthy parenting. There is no perfect parent.

So, where did you go wrong? That's the question that haunts many now aged parents when they are experiencing abuse and control from their now-grown child. Of course, hindsight is always 20-20. We can all look back and see various things we would change, but the reality is, we cannot change the past, nor should we even attempt to. It is wasteful of time and energy. Focusing on the present is more important. Like many young parents, you gave your children what your parents gave you, making some adjustments along the way based on the knowledge and experience you've gained in life. Unquestionably, if you would have known better, you would have been better. Therefore, your biggest mistake was probably ignorance.

As your child got older and you witnessed their unhealthy behaviors, you most likely became frustrated and angry because you did not know what to do. At that point, you probably began enabling their behavior by not setting boundaries. As your frustration grew, you most likely said and did some things that you've come to regret. Then at some point, you most likely succumbed to their controlling tactics, thinking you could fix them or 'right the wrongs' of the past by complying with their wishes and giving in to their demands, hoping they'd come to the understanding that you love them. However, that only kicked the can down the road, and at some point, you will arrive at the crossroad where the wounded, now grown adult child will manifest his or her pain onto you. Whatever you did to them that was unhealthy, ask them for forgiveness, repent to God, and move forward in your life. You don't owe them anything anymore. They are responsible for their healing and deliverance.

Controlling Religious Leaders

The spirit of Jezebel and control lavishes itself in many of our religious institutions and is seen in leaders. This spirit will manifest in an extraordinarily authoritarian and uncompromisingly controlling leader. Many of these leaders are narcissists; however, some are just controlling. Regardless of which it is, it is causing damage to the lives of many people. They struggle significantly in their own identity and look to the pulpit, position, and titles to strengthen their flawed identity. Pride and rejection are at the core of leaders that are controlling. Many of these religious tycoons engage in controlling witchcraft that significantly damages those that come to the church or church leader for help. That is indeed a travesty.

Religious leaders such as Apostles, Prophets, Evangelists, Pastors, Teachers, Elders, Bishops, Reverends, and Priest are people just like everyone else. They experience trauma, pain, and they may be dysfunctional in some areas or be emotionally disconnected. As such, they need deliverance and the subsequent renewing of the mind to be in a position to lead effectively. Leaders are held to a higher standard.

Not many of you should become teachers (self-constituted censors and reprovers of others), my brethren, for you know that we [teachers] will be judged by a higher standard and with greater severity than other people; thus, we assume the greater accountability and the more condemnation - James 3:1 AMPC

So, what behaviors does a controlling religious leader demonstrate? You must be aware that the controlling religious spirit is linked to the controlling political and corrupt nature that exists within various nations and communities. Controlling leaders will use nepotism and bring family and friends into positions they are not qualified to have. Additionally, controlling religious leaders will often overlook the sins within their leadership team, including their family members who are in the ministry. Essentially the controlling religious spirit creates a system of the good old boys. Of course, this is all part of Jezebel's web of destruction. Innocent people looking for help put a tremendous amount of trust and faith in these leaders. It is here where things begin to spiral out of control.

Controlling leaders keep a short leash on the flock. They cannot let go of the reins as they most likely fear the gifts and anointing found in other people. They rarely trust anyone and look to maintain control at all costs. They either need to make all the decisions or sign off on everything. Nothing can be done without the leader's permission. This toxic behavior looks to control the personal life of church members. For example, a leader may tell a church member that they cannot go on vacation as they are needed at the church to serve. Invading personal lives, the decisions and choices that people make is out of order and controlling.

Controlling churches and leaders have unbalanced teaching in the area of submission and authority. They will twist and wrangle scriptures on this topic to get you to submit to their every command and serve them. Additionally, controlling leaders are never wrong. The decisions they make are regularly projected to others as God speaking directly to them. God certainly speaks to his people, but he doesn't only talk to the leader. However, the toxic, controlling leader will manipulate scripture to get you to think that somehow, he or she, as the leader, has a higher ranking in the spirit than you. That is demonic and has brought much damage to many decent people of faith.

Controlling leaders treat their followers more like slaves, then citizens of God's kingdom. They rarely empower others to serve in a capacity whereby the entire body is blessed. Any incoming and aspiring preacher or minister is forced to serve sometimes for years before they ever have the opportunity to release the gift of God that is within them. Controlling Pastors will diminish you to an "armor-bearer," a term that has been thrown out by many controlling pastors. These "armor-bearers" many times are nothing more than personal servants to the selfish and controlling Pastor.

Controlling leaders and ministries alike will intimidate and manipulate their congregation as well. For example, they will curse people if they leave the church. They look to project a tremendous amount of shame, guilt, and fear on believers that leave the ministry. Some leaders will make shocking statements such as 'the hand of God will depart from your life if you leave.' They will also tell people within the congregation to stay away from those who have left the church. There may be times when they will inform church members not to be around their family members because they are not part of the church or deemed by leadership as troublemakers.

Controlling leaders forbid you from attending or visiting any other church other than theirs. At times you must get the leaders' permission' to go to conferences that they do not host. Controlling leaders will also say that they are the only true church and that everyone else is a fraud.

Additionally, believers who are not in attendance every week or do not donate to the ministry as the leader sees fit may become the subject of the leader's sermon. This is designed to embarrass and humiliate you to the point where you comply with their wishes. Unfortunately, these kindhearted people are portrayed to others as demons or as rebellious and unfaithful members.

Finally, controlling leaders will reject any type of questioning you have relative to what they are doing. When you bring up a question or an issue, you're immediately shut down and potentially demonize.

If you're under the spell of a controlling leader or religious network, you are in a dangerous position. Seek deliverance and counseling immediately.

Controlling Tactics

The abuser's objective is to control, whereas the tactics are how they will accomplish their purpose. You must become aware of the various tactics that controllers use. The controller wants to keep you from educating yourself regarding unhealthy behaviors and identifying potential abusers.

While there are many tactics that a controlling person would use, the following represent just a sample of some of them.

Manipulation

The goal of manipulation to a controller is to get what they want and gain dominance and influence. However, they also use manipulation to abuse their intended targets through mind games that distort reality and emotional exploitation design to influence your behavior.

Controllers know your weakness and will use those weaknesses against you. Watch for chronic emotional manipulation where blame, complaints, pouting, crying, and intentional passive/aggressive behavior are utilized to weaken your boundaries and destabilize your emotions. Additional manipulative tactics can include withholding information, withholding sex or affection, lying, twisting the truth, and explosive outbursts that provide you with ultimatums, whereby you eventually cave into the demands of the controller.

However, manipulation may not always be intentional. Many people don't know that they are manipulative. Regardless, it's very important to remember that you must specifically identify and describe the manipulation and how you feel regarding it when someone manipulates you, whether the person is a controller or not.

Criticism

Controllers will use criticism to make you feel inadequate and devalued. The controller will criticize your every decision. Controllers will disapprove of you and your actions no matter how well you behave. Jezebelic controllers search out those that have been hurt before, whether by a spouse, a parent, friend, or associate; if you've been wounded or have a poor self-image, the controller will capitalize on this.

Whatever you do, don't think that you can tame the controller with perfect behavior. It's virtually guaranteed that the controller will find a fault in you and what you do. Controllers may hide their criticism by stating that they are constructive in their criticism of you or your actions. This lie is designed to gain some level of trust from you. Controllers never look to build you up. They are always looking for ways to tear you down and achieve some level of preeminence.

On the flip side, a controller does not handle criticism well at all. Their fragile core requires them to set up an internal wall designed to explode at the moment of criticism. Narcissistic controllers are always looking to gain admiration from people. To them, they are perfect, and everyone outside of them are failures and inferior to them. Criticism threatens their view of themself, and they will typically lash out at the one that criticizes them. This lashing out usually is very severe and will immediately deploy defensive flares of aggressive manifestations ranging from verbal assaults to potential physical harm.

Isolation

Controllers will both isolate themselves and their victims as necessary, many times running in and out of both tactics simply to keep others off balance. They will isolate themselves as a means of punishing their victims. That usually occurs when the controller is challenged and called out for their abusive behavior. They will run and hide, not answering phone calls or personal home visits. That is part of the push-pull tactic within the gaslighting dimension. It's designed to get you to invite them back into your life. Don't fall for it -move on with your life.

Controllers will isolate those they're in a relationship with by forbidding them to see friends or family or participate in outside activities such as the church or going to the gym to work out. They will go as far as controlling who you talk to on the phone, and they will monitor all social media postings. Remember, the controller demands loyalty, and if you don't give it, they will take it by isolating you to themselves.

Silent Treatment

Controllers will also use passive tactics, such as the silent treatment against you. It is not uncommon for a controller to position you for further torment down the road by going silent with you for the duration they deem necessary to bring you to a place of needing or desiring them to return either into a relationship or open up communication with them.

Making you wait

Controllers are also notorious for trying to control time – your time! They will intentionally be late for special events that you are emotionally involved in. Things like birthdays, weddings, Thanksgiving, and Christmas are some of the examples. While you wait, they will have you on 'pins and needles' as you journey on your emotional rollercoaster. Being chronically late, making false promises and appointments are all ways to gain or maintain control.

If and when they do show up, if you have moved forward with your event without them, the controller will meet you with intense drama and attacks of blame. You will be blamed for not reminding them, or if you did remind them, not reminding them enough times. They will blame someone else, insinuating that they were "held-up" because they had to deal with someone else's problem.

Catastrophizing

Catastrophizing happens when someone makes a catastrophe out of a situation or makes something seem far worse than it is. Controllers always project the worst possible outcome in any situation. Catastrophizing is sometimes referred to as "over-reacting." Controllers consistently over-react have an array of motivations for catastrophizing, including drawing attention to themselves or away from an issue or produce a specific reaction from the person(s) they are controlling.

Controllers are highly dramatic and always exaggerate. They have numerous things that they're doing that are so big that you should help them out. The purpose of this is to pull you in and pass you their famous 'ball of confusion.'

Revenge

A controller is typically not going to let anything that was done to them, that diminishes their selfish view of self, or their control of others go unchecked. If you did anything to a controller in the past, they would look to bring vengeance against you to display their dominance.

If you ever break your commitment to someone narcissistic or controlling, there will be retaliation against you in the form of manipulation. It's designed to get you to operate against your will and line up with the controller's agenda. Controllers are never concerned about your choices but only their evil plots of torment against you.

Retaliation works in many ways. In some cases, it will be forceful and immediate. In others, it may be slow and progressive. Retaliatory tactics may include sabotage and gossip. Sabotage tactics may consist of financial attacks designed to impair your ability to live life in a healthy manner. Vindictive and vicious attacks against your personal property and career are not uncommon for the controller. Gossip, slander, and instigating rumors among your friends and family will also be used as a means to obtain revenge against you. Remember, the controller is a type of terrorist in the spirit and the psyche of a person.

Labeling

Controllers like to use labels to frustrate you and stir up your emotions, specifically anger. Choice words of negativity laced with well-timed accusations will create the impression that fault rests entirely with you. Labels such as "immature," "demon," "coward," or "hater" are particularly useful in creating 'smoke-screens' that camouflage their narcissistic and controlling behaviors that hurt you.

They may also label you a Jezebel or Narcissist. This is called 'flipping' and its purpose is to bring you into a passive posture whereby you coil up and withdraw from challenging their behavior.

Asking why

"Why didn't you do your part?" or "Why were you late?" "Why didn't you call me?"

On the surface, these may seem like legitimate and straightforward questions - they could be. However, with a controller, it can be a tactic used to control. Asking why is designed to accomplish two primary things. One, it's designed to gain information from you. It's a type of reconnaissance or intelligence gathering to find out your business. Ultimately this will be used against you in the form of the abuser controlling and dominating you. Secondly, it intends to have you think that somehow you don't know what you're doing or are a terrible person. That is designed to remind you that you don't matter and to devalue your self-esteem. Many times, this is combined with sarcasm.

Sarcasm

Sarcasm is an excellent way of saying something hurtful without taking any responsibility for it. Sarcasm makes someone feel worthless or inferior. A controller will use sarcasm to gain superiority. Sarcasm is a covert way to take little jabs at people. An example of sarcasm would be if someone says something obvious, and the sarcastic remark would be, "well, you're the sharpest knife in the drawer." Don't fall for the lies of the controller that suggests that their little digs were harmless. Sarcasm is not benign. The narcissistic controller intends to bring harm through a multitude of tactics, including sarcasm.

Timing

A controller usually picks an inopportune time to argue or express some feelings that they have towards you. They will call you, text you, or show up at your door late at night, or while you're watching your favorite TV show or right before you have an appointment. Watch for controllers showing up at the time you least expect. They do this so they can find you when you're worn out, exhausted, tired, or have suffered some type of physical or mental stress.

Casting Guilt

Controllers look to cast guilt upon their intended victims. Guilt is a feeling of a violation of one's values or beliefs. For example, "my behavior was bad." Many of these controllers come from a place of shame where their view of self is not good. As such, they need to make you feel that you have done something wrong when indeed, it is them that has done something wrong. This tactic is designed to once again control and, of course, dominate the relationship.

Narcissistic controllers will guilt you into getting what they want. That is the sole purpose of casting guilt on you. If you are the type of person that is always looking to be excepted by others or a people pleaser, a controller will undoubtedly look to cast guilt on you to manipulate you into getting what they want.

Additionally, a controlling Jezebel and narcissist will use one's faith and religious beliefs to guilt them into acting a certain way. They may manipulate scriptures and share them with you to guilt you to do something that they want. They may even say that "God told you to _____ for me, but you are disobedient." They may also twist and wrangle scripture and saying things like, "the Bible says that if I ask you for your coat, you should give me your cloak also," implying that you should give them the shirt off your back to them. Of course, this is often referred to as narcissistic projection, witchcraft, and religious control.

Confusion

Controllers love to play mind games and will use confusion to bring you into submission to their will. Controllers will use irrational comments, statements, or discussions that leave you confused about the situation at hand. That is designed to have you question your sanity. It is a form of gaslighting that controller uses against its victims. The Bible says,

For where envying and strife is, there is confusion and every evil work. James 3:16

Controllers often change their minds and requests according to their impulse. They will demand something one minute and then may require the exact opposite shortly after that. That is designed to keep you off balance and confused. You practically don't know if you're coming or going.

For God is not the author of confusion but of peace, as in all the churches of the saints. 1 Corinthians 14:33

Controllers will turn the table on you when you have questions or concerns about something. For example, if you ask a question, they typically will not give you a straight answer, or they may completely fabricate something. This will most likely be extraordinarily agitating and frustrating for you as you attempt to have a rational discussion. The controller manifests by blaming you, even suggesting that you were causing conflict. More than likely, they will begin to use a technique called 'word salad.' Word salad is a form of speech that introduces confusing or random words and phrases. Much of this is designed to leave you in a state of confusion, scratching your head and wondering what happened.

Using money and resources

Controllers will also use money and gift-giving as a means to create a tether to bring your guard down. The Bible tells us to protect our hearts.

Keep thy heart with all diligence; for out of it are the issues of life. - Proverbs 4:23

The heart is your subconscious mind and must be protected from invading forces looking to plant seeds of doubt, fear, insecurity, low self-esteem, hopelessness, and depression.

When a controller gives you money, gifts, or does favors for you, there are typically strings attached. Watch for controllers giving you money at strange times or buying you gifts to butter you up. Be aware that controllers will do pleasant things for you. For example, they will buy you gifts, pay for a vacation, and drop off groceries at your house for the sole purpose of getting you to feel comfortable around them. The controllers desire to get you to feel relaxed with them and open yourself up. Gift-giving is another form of control and manipulation that a controller will use to get you to feel obligated to communicate with them. Gifts are given to have the targeted victim compromise the truth and not confront the controller's insidious spirit and dysfunctional behavior.

Controllers will keep a tight grip on financial resources. They will control access to accounts, keeping you from making withdraws and buying things. This keeps you economically dependent on them and makes it much more difficult for you to exit the relationship.

Squatting

While we do not necessarily use this term based on its precise definition, we use it to explain another tactic that a controller will use. A controller will squat and live in your home, apartment, or camp out on your property if possible, and when you want them to leave - they don't. They will begin to argue with you, stating that they somehow have a right to be there.

Although they pay no rent, contribute nothing to the home but rather create stress, strife, and confusion, they 'park' themselves there. Of course, the purpose of doing this is to aggravate you, frustrate you and eventually control you. You can try to speak in a cordial/diplomatic and sensible way, but it usually does not work with a controller. As such, as the property owner, you must follow the state's eviction laws where the property is located and get them out!

Using your address

This tactic is similar to them living with you, yet they don't live with you; they just use your address. Frankly, controllers will use multiple addresses, and many times will have numerous aliases. Remember, the controller is executing a controlling mind game. When they use your address, they're strategizing that if and when they're in your home, and you ask them to leave, they will simply tell the authorities that my mail goes there, and as such, I have a right to be there. While that's not necessarily true; it does create some complications and difficulties when you attempt to get them out of your home.

Additionally, if their mail is coming to your residence, they can have their driver's license or other official documents be associated with your address. If they are a corrupt person or running various scams and shams, you may find the police knocking on your door one day looking for them. If you ask them to change their address, you might be met with a fury of attacks and blame. Furthermore, they will accuse you of taking their mail or hiding it from them. Of course, this is not true, but it's another way to bring about confusion, shower you with blame and keep the tension at a level that makes you want to give up.

Storing stuff

Here's another tactic that seems very harmless, yet it can be extremely damaging to your emotional well-being—storing personal property on your lot or in your home. It usually starts as something simple, like can I store a box in your garage. Over time this becomes problematic as they begin to add more and more stuff. They will often park their car in front of your house, or if they have an RV and your lot is big enough, they will leave it there potentially for years. It doesn't matter if the car or the RV works; they will leave it, as unsightly as it is, at your dwelling place. Of course, at some point, you're going to become frustrated, disgusted, and eventually angry about all of this 'stuff' that has gathered at your residence. Again, you can ask them kindly to remove it, but there's always some drama or excuse why they can't, and they will even say that they have a right to do it or that somehow you owe them and must comply with their wishes. That is control and its finest.

If you try to get rid of it, you can't. It's unsightly, and you trigger some level of frustration or anger every time you see it. You may not consider it a big deal; however, the controller does things with a strategy and purpose. This tactic is to make you feel obligated and create a bond between you and them. It's as if you cannot get them out of your head. Why? Because every time you see their 'stuff,' you're reminded of their behavior, their drama, and you ultimately become tormented in your mind and emotions.

Shape-shifting behavior

Many times, the controller will combine passive with aggressive behavior. This is a unique way of voicing anger without directly expressing the emotion. You see this often in covert narcissists.

Shapeshifters often display a Jekyll and Hyde type behavior, kind and caring one-minute (Dr. Jekyll) and angry and rageful (Mr. Hyde) the next. Shape-shifting controllers can be depressed and isolated, seeing themselves as the victim. Then they transition into a dominating and hyper-aggressive person that's going to show you who is boss.

When a controller shape-shifts, they take your emotions on a roller coaster ride of abuse of toxic proportions. They are aggressively positioning themselves to control your life. A person that is passive/aggressive can be very dangerous.

Blaming

There's another widespread tactic of a person who is looking to control others -blaming. Casting blaming on others is making it clear that fault lies entirely with the other person.

Controllers blame so they can create the illusion that they are simply the innocent victim. They will never admit that their behavior played any part in the difficulty; instead, they make sure that you realize that you need to change in the relationship – not them. Why? Because with the controller, it's all your fault!

Blame shifting

Blame shifting, which is a part of gaslighting, is another strategy that people who need to control engage in. It gives them a sense of being powerful and in control. Controllers target emotionally unstable people, typically those who do not know how to manage their emotions properly or feel worthy of having good healthy boundaries. Blame shifting is designed for a person to question themselves, their thoughts, and their feelings. The controller will often become verbally and emotionally aggressive and look you square in the face and say, 'it's all your fault.'

If you are not an emotionally stable person, then blame-shifting will immediately become the evidence to support your low view of self. You must increase your emotional intelligence and set healthy boundaries so that you can be prepared for this quick, '*shift on the fly*' blame.

Mind-reading

Controllers are notorious for using this tactic, which is part of the gaslighting protocol. Mind reading is when another person thinks they know what the other person is thinking, feeling, and how they will respond and react to situations. For example, the controller may say, "You did that for me because you want something from me," or "You don't really feel that way." These are all exceptionally effective at bringing confusion and controlling the topic or relationship.

Mind reading is a type of projection of one's will onto another by wrongly assuming what another person feels, thinks, or expects. Controllers will tell you that they know the real reason why you act a certain way. It is designed to devalue and ultimately dismiss any issue you have.

Intimidation

Controllers use intimidation tactics to suppress you, shut you down, and incite fear. Fear brings torment and causes one to make hasty and unwise decisions. Of course, that's what the controller wants. Controllers prey on fear. Like a dog, they can sense your fear. When you are fearful of their tactics, they gain the advantage.

Intimidation can manifest in various ways. The key is to be aware of the tactics the controller typically uses. Once you are aware, you are no longer ignorant of their methods. The Bible instructs us that we should not be unaware of how the enemy operates, or else we give the advantage to our opponent.

lest Satan should take advantage of us; for we are not ignorant of his devices - 2 Corinthians 2:11

By mentally preparing yourself ahead of time, you'll be better equipped to deal with any intimidation tactic, ultimately dismissing it as a powerless weapon in the controller's inventory of toxic behaviors. Remember, it is the intention of the one who is doing the intimidating to frighten you to the point where you do what they want. Controllers use intimidation to get you to think that they are superior to you. Coercion is essentially an attempt to persuade someone to do something by using force or threats. This threat may be made privately or in public settings. But again, at the end of the day, it wants you to fear it.

Elevating their Voice

Another way that controllers look to intimidate their prey is by elevating their voice. They project their voice loudly and aggressively while expressing negative emotions. This tactic is often used to pressure you to submit to their bullying tactic, ultimately giving them what they want. They will often combine threatening body language with their aggressive voice to increase the effectiveness of this tactic. For example, standing over you or staring you down to make you feel uncomfortable can be used by them to intimidate you. Suppose they are physically stronger or taller, or their physique is much larger. In that case, they will use that in combination with their elevated voice to gain the advantage so they can control the discussion and dominate you.

Flying Monkey's

Controllers are notorious for having a broad array of people at their disposal to execute their plans. When the controller wants to punish you, they will release their assassins known as "flying monkeys."

Controllers gain support from other people that they have seduced into siding with them. These 'flying monkeys' are strategically used as pawns in the chess game of control. Controllers will connect with others and establish a relationship with them, whereby they can be used as 'flying monkeys' to attack you. This is referred to as "ganging up" on you.

Flying monkeys will use various tactics such as guilt-tripping, twisting the truth, gaslighting, verbal assaults, threats, and at times violence. Flying monkeys Will bring messages from the controller. Sometimes these messages come lined with guilt, while other times, they ask that you forgive and embrace the controller. Don't take the bait!

Narcissistic controllers are very good at creating an image of themself that they are the victim. They are consistently cornering other people and badmouthing others, suggesting somehow that they are the victim in the relationship. They're often able to seduce people due to their charm, charisma, or false humility. Once they gain enough supporters, they will strategically set in motion a hurricane of attacks against you. In many cases, this war leaves you feeling as if the world has collapsed on you, and nobody supports you. This can lead to depression, loneliness, hopelessness, and despair. All of this is what the controller wants to happen. At some point, don't be surprised if the controller tries to rescue you from your misery. They won't necessarily do this directly; they will deploy flying monkeys to put the seed in your mind that they're not the bad guy. Don't take the bait; pull yourself up from your bootstraps, strengthen yourself, and learn how to deal with a controller and his or her assassins.

Misplaced Control

Are you a person who has an unquenchable desire to control things out of your control or fix something that is not your responsibility? If so, you may be operating with misplaced control.

Perhaps you want to help a troubled family member - a mother, father, husband, wife, an adult child, or maybe even a very good friend. But what if they do not want your help, but yet you consistently force yourself into their situation because somehow you think that you need to be in control of it or fix it? Maybe it's a good friend who is going through a bad relationship. You find yourself trying to save that friend from the problems their experiencing.

What about things like the political temperature of the country where you live? Can you control who wins or loses an election? Do you find yourself taking on heavy burdens that drive you to participate in matters that do not pertain to you? Do you consistently say within yourself that I need to be involved in issues because "*if I don't get involved, it will be a disaster?*" Or possibly you find yourself troubled from attempting to help someone who is blind to the fact that they are in a toxic and abusive relationship but yet will not make decisions; therefore, you must take control and make decisions for them. If so, you're probably attempting to control something that you simply cannot control - this is referred to as misplaced control.

Misplaced control is when we control things that we can't control while ignoring what we can and often should control.

When something is misplaced, it is incorrectly positioned. We have all at one point or another 'misplaced' something—for example, a set of keys, or our wallet, or perhaps a critical document. When things are misplaced, they are somewhere – just not where they are supposed to be. Control can be misplaced when we focus on what we can't change while ignoring what we can.

When facing any challenging situation, ask yourself a series of questions:

1) What can I control?
2) What can't I control?
3) What should I control?
4) What shouldn't I control?

We cannot control many things—for example, the weather, the stock market, and of course, other people. However, we can and should control our own choices and behaviors. People need to focus on their own decisions and actions rather than on those of others. We should never control other people.

Mis-placed control can also have you susceptible to gossip and talebearing. Some people feel they must hear others' stories and problems so they can be the one that has the answer and make everything right. That is called being 'the fixer.' A person with a fixer spirit is a controlling person that is possibly operating with a Jezebel spirit. Mis-placed control can initially make you feel good about yourself. However, it is a false sense of security. When one comes to others' aid, they feel good about themselves that they have really 'helped.' A chronic mis-placed controller (i.e., fixer) is typically birthed out of rejection, shame, abandonment, and insecurity.

Stay in your lane

When driving your car on a highway, it is essential to stay in your lane. When one does not stay in their lane but instead veers into someone else's lane, it can be catastrophic. Not staying in your lane can cause accidents. It's the same way in life, specifically with relationships with other people. It's important to remember to stay in your lane and mind your own business. When we want to get involved in someone else's life and fix their problems, it's then that we can become a controller. Staying in your lane means letting the other person experience life to grow and develop and learn to fail in a healthy manner.

It is essential to understand that loving and supporting others does not mean that we need to rescue or fix their problems. It is very dangerous when we equate love and support with fixing and saving. Seeing a family member, especially a now-grown child or a longtime friend struggling or suffering in some area; it can be natural to want to help. We must remain empathetic but, at the same time, understand that there are boundaries that we should not violate. Sometimes people just need space and time to work out the issues of life for themselves. It does not make you an evil person to watch from a distance someone else processing their issues. It's important to remember that you should not run to the aid of someone else at the first sign of seeing them having some difficulty or finding them in an uncomfortable position in their life.

Additionally, getting involved in and attempting to fix other people's business can hinder your forward progress. Many need to learn to mind their own business. If you concentrate and focus on your personal affairs, your relationships, and your issues, then there would be a lot less stress in your life, and you'll accomplish much more. When you stay in your lane, you are a healthy person.

Misplaced control expends a massive amount of energy. You only have so much time and energy. Trying to control other people's circumstances, situations, and decisions are wasting time and energy. Stay in your lane and mind your own matters. Work on yourself and stop trying to control others. Focus your energy on what you *can* control. When we focus on what we can't control, such as other people's decisions or dysfunction, we become drained. Trying to force our lives into what we think others should be is misplaced control.

Coupled with misplaced control is False Responsibility. Many are stressed and have a tremendous amount of anxiety due to feeling responsible for things they are not responsible for or cannot control.

False responsibility

False responsibility is when a person feels responsible for fixing everyone's problems yet ignore their needs. These are the ones that pass out life jackets to everyone, yet they never put one on themselves. Perhaps a good analogy to give would be similar to when you take a flight on a plane. Before takeoff, the flight attendants will provide instructions over the intercom system. One of the things that they say is that an oxygen mask will fall in the event of a loss of cabin pressure. They then state that if you are traveling with a small child, you should take the mask and put it on yourself first and then attend to the little child's needs. This is because you cannot help others when you are in need of life support.

Jesus talks about trying to fix other people's problems when you have your own things to deal with.

Hypocrite! First get rid of the log in your own eye; then you will see well enough to deal with the speck in your friend's eye
Matthew 7:5 NLT

Additionally, Jesus gives Peter a candid response when Peter sticks his nose in someone else's business by asking, "what's going to happen to John?" Jesus brushes off the question and says, "*What is that to you?*" (i.e., "None of your business")

When Peter saw him behind them, he asked Jesus, "Lord, what about him?" Jesus answered, "If I want him to live until I come back, that is not your business. You follow me." John 21:21-22 NCV

False responsibility stems from a syndrome known as codependency. A codependent person focuses more on the problems of other people than their issues. In many cases, this is a subconscious stronghold built to avoid addressing one's issues. If you need to be involved in other people's problems to feel good about yourself, you probably are in bondage to a spirit of false responsibility.

False responsibility is a burden that stems from being rejected, shamed, blamed, and a burden of guilt being placed on you, specifically when you were in your developmental years, approximately 0 to 8 years old. During these years and through these gateways, demonic spirits can keep one in a place of bondage to false responsibility.

False responsibility uses others' needs to meet your need for acceptance by doing for others what they should be doing for themselves. It is essentially tied to control as you take on the false responsibility to rescue, fix, or save other people.

You may suffer from false responsibility if you:

- Feel Guilty if you don't do something
- Feel as if your happiness depends on other people
- Would instead attend to the issues of others than your issues
- Find yourself trying to "save the day"
- Inclined to take on the moods of people close to you
- Are overly sensitive to criticism
- Tend to get "caught up" in other people's problems
- Feel responsible for the feelings of others

What are we responsible for?

We are responsible for our behaviors, choices, problems, attitudes, happiness, character defects, thoughts, feelings, mistakes, and how we treat others. We are also responsible for our thoughts and our emotions. Additionally, we are responsible for whether or not we allow others to abuse, manipulate, or mistreat us. You can't blame others for what you permit or enable.

We are not responsible for other people's choices, behaviors, bad decisions, addictions, the consequences of their choices, hopes, dreams, character defects, thoughts, feelings, problems, attitudes, and moods. We are responsible for ourselves; we are not responsible for others.

Does this mean we do not care about others? Of course not. When appropriate, and if the situation warrants it, we most certainly need to care for others. However, it must be done in a healthy manner.

In Galatians 6:2, Paul the apostle states that we should:

Bear ye one another's burdens, and so fulfil the law of Christ.

Paul further goes on to state in Galatians 6:5

Let every man bear his own burden.

So, which is it? Do we take someone's burden or not? From a biblical standpoint, the answer is found in the meaning of the word' *burden.*' In verse 2, the word burden speaks of something that was not due to someone's action, behavior, or decision. It's talking more about something that was out of the person's control. For example, if a tornado comes in and levels your home, it is the community's responsibility to carry that burden. You didn't ask for it, nor did you do anything to cause it; it was merely a matter of natural disaster.

However, in verse 5, the word burden does not mean the same thing. Here, it is the word '*load.*' and refers to something created by you that you are responsible for and have an obligation to address. An example would be someone irresponsible in credit card spending. They overspent and now cannot pay their rent or their light bill. In this example, it is not the community's responsibility or others to come in and rescue them. That '*burden*' (load) belongs to the person who created it. This corresponds with the principle of sowing and reaping. If you sow it - you will reap it.

Taking on false responsibility to fix other people can become extremely destructive to genuine and authentic self-identity. Taking on others' responsibility can also be a sign that others must approve you to be worthy. There is a fear of being rejected that puts a massive demand on self whereby you expect yourself to perform so well that you win others' approval. Of course, this is an irrational belief that must be replaced with a rational thought that states, "I am valuable simply as a human being, and I permit myself to be my authentic self.

Misplaced control and false responsibility have significant emotional and behavioral consequences. Depression, anxiety, fear of failing, fear of being embarrassed, fear of rejection, fear of being judged, and feeling bad about yourself are some of the emotional consequences.

Some behaviors that provoke false responsibility are chronic self-criticism, self-accusation, procrastination, workaholism, people-pleasing, and the inability to express or embrace your true self. If you see a pattern in your relationships that reveal that you are consistently trying to fix others and their situation or, control the outcome of their decisions, in that case, seek professional life coaching and counselling as you require deliverance healing and wholeness.

Breaking Free from the Controller

Technically other people cannot control you. Control is not something that is taken but instead is something that is relinquished. Control is power handed over. That is why we must be on guard to retain control of ourselves at all costs.

To emancipate and liberate yourself from controlling people, organizations, systems, and cultures, you must understand that you have a choice. You must choose to be in control of yourself.

Remember, if you are being controlled by anyone or anything, it is because you have permitted it. Why? Because you have some form of need. Some of these needs may be the:

1) need for approval
2) need for acceptance
3) need for appreciation
4) need for people to like you
5) need for people to be pleased with you
6) need for people to be happy
7) need to be validated
8) need to be with a person
9) need to fix the person
10) need for people to praise you

There are several techniques you can use to liberate yourself from controllers. However, due to the uniqueness of the controlling operation, there is no one-size-fits-all application. The following represent some things you can do to get free from controlling relationships.

#1 Come out of denial

The first thing you can do is come out from any self-denying that you are being controlled or are in a controlling relationship. Denial is not that you don't know the truth. Denial is that you know the truth or the facts; you simply just choose to ignore them. To come out of denial means to embrace reality and take control of your life. A controller's behavior should be enough evidence to suggest that the person is a controller. And yes, this can be hard; it can be tough to accept the truth that your loved one is a controller. But once you relax and take a moment to think about the person's actual behavior, you'll see that they have gained control over your life.

Check your own emotions. How do you feel? Do you feel tense, stressed, and tormented with fear every time the person's number pops up on your phone, or they show up at your house? Do you find yourself avoiding them at all cost? If so, it's most likely that they are a controller. That does not mean that you don't have some issues and things you need to work on yourself. You do. However, the first step in getting free from a controller is acknowledging that they are indeed controlling you.

Stop hiding from the fact that you are in a relationship with a control-freak. Regardless of how much you want to think of them as a good person, it cannot come at the expense of denying the truth of their behavior. They need help but denying that the problem exists is not going to help the situation. Frankly, it's going to create additional opportunities for you to be controlled not only by the person you're presently in a relationship with but down the road as well. Further denial will create a vast porthole over your life that attracts more dysfunctional people into your life.

Making a hard decision to establish boundaries in your life or limit interaction or going no contact with a person can bring about anxiety. Nonetheless, it is a decision that needs to be made. Denial can be a coping mechanism that keeps you away from addressing the situation at hand. So, you need to come face-to-face with your denial. If you do not, you will remain bound in multiple areas of your life, specifically to and with the controller.

Signs that you're in denial

- You dismiss the topic when somebody brings up the fact that you are being controlled
- You don't want to talk about the potential that you're being controlled
- You become anxious, defensive, or agitated when other people bring up that the person is controlling you
- You avoid talking to friends or family members who are warning you of the control in the person you're in a relationship with
- You dismiss the control by introducing hyper-spiritual ideologies suggesting that being with that controlling person (or organization) is "your ministry."
- You continue to say to yourself, "it's fine, and it will eventually go away."

To get free from denial, you need to identify any irrational beliefs that you may have. Specifically, the irrational belief that you must be approved and connected to other people to be considered worthy. That belief must be replaced with a new rational view that validates and suggests that you are worthy simply because you are God's creation. Lastly, you must learn to desire love from only those who appreciate you and recognize the good in you. If you have this mindset, controllers will most likely not be attracted to you.

#2 Establish healthy boundaries

It is imperative that when addressing controlling people that you establish healthy boundaries for yourself. Quite frankly, had boundaries been established and communicated early in the relationship, you most likely would not have remained in a controlling relationship. Even if those boundaries were violated (by the controller), then your corresponding consequences would have activated, and you would have divested from the relationship.

It's essential to begin by discussing just exactly what a healthy boundary is not. A border is not a wall that you put up. When people have experienced emotional pain or wounds, they have a propensity to build up walls in their life. These walls are self-sabotage as they do not provide the person the freedom to give love correctly or receive love.

People that do not establish boundaries are generally viewed as limitless, weak, and unstable by the controllers. Not having boundaries essentially gives them "permission" to manipulate you. However, once you establish your boundaries and communicate your limits, the controller will become frustrated.

Saying no to the controller will move from the controlling person to a frustrating person.

What is a boundary?

So just exactly what is a boundary? A boundary is similar to a fence or property line. If you have a fence around your home, you are letting people know that this is where they should stop - they don't have a right to enter. If they enter then, that is trespassing because it's your property, not theirs. When trespassing on someone else's property, there can be consequences, some of them quite severe.

Personal boundaries protect you by setting a clear line between you and other people. It is important to remember that it is your responsibility to set boundaries for your life rather than other people. Healthy boundaries never place demands on or control other people, but rather is designed solely to protect one's personal space. When establishing your boundaries, it's important to communicate those boundaries, especially with the controller. Remember, boundaries not expressed are no boundaries at all. Be prepared to share your boundaries consistently. Make it a habit to refresh the boundaries with the controller. That will let them know you are serious about where their life stops and yours begins.

Additionally, be prepared for them to retaliate against your boundaries with theirs. Let them know you respect their boundary for their life, and as such, they need to respect yours. Any control or threats they communicate, which they mistake for a boundary, must be met with correction. Simply remind them that a border never places demands or controls other people, but rather is designed to protect one's personal space.

Not expressing or communicating your boundaries says, "I have no limits." That could potentially be very dangerous, especially in relationships. If you have no boundaries in a relationship, you're signaling to others that you don't know how to take care of yourself. That leaves you open to attracting people who want to control. It can also lead to mental, emotional, physical, or sexual abuse by others against you.

When boundaries are violated, there must always be a consequence of that violation. Again, a boundary must be viewed as a fence. Some fences have barbed wire on top of the fence. The purpose of that is to discourage outsiders from invading that property and let them know that there will be consequences if they try. And if they disregard the razor-sharp barbed wire fence (the boundary) and attempt to climb over it and get cut, it is not the fault of the property owner who put up the fence. They didn't cut you; you cut yourself. The same holds for people who violate personal boundaries. Whatever the consequences, it is not you are doing anything to them. They did it to themselves.

Concerning personal boundaries that are violated, an example of a consequence might be going temporary no contact or severing the relationship. That is an area that many people struggle with and for many reasons. One of the most significant obstacles with "cutting the cord" with people is the view that it somehow equates to the lack of love. Making healthy choices for yourself by establishing firm boundaries and deploying the consequences of violated boundaries is not a lack of love towards other people. On the contrary, it is an expression of love towards our creator (God), your neighbor, and yourself.

Remember, it's your boundary that you're establishing, so you can set it any way you desire. Just remember you set boundaries for your life. You cannot nor should not set boundaries for other people's lives. If you do that, you become the controller.

#3 "No Contact"

The term no contact refers to a principal where you don't call, receive calls, text, or email the controlling person any longer. That can potentially include other family members and friends that they could manipulate and get on their side. When deploying the no contact rule, do not ask mutual friends to give the person you are in no contact with a message. Additionally, when going no contact, you may need to change your cell phone number. You will need to block specific phone numbers from gaining access to you. You can do the same with your email accounts and other social media portals. It is advisable that on social media that you 'unfriend" and block the controller and the controllers flying monkeys from seeing your posts or posting to your wall. You will also need to exercise some level of self-discipline. Refrain from visiting the controller's social media pages or wonder what they're doing. The purpose of no-contact is to stabilize you and bring peace into your life.

Going no contact with someone you genuinely love or a family member can be extremely frustrating and painful. However, it is not as painful as being abused by the controlling person. Remember, this is a fight for your mind and emotions.

Whether the relationship is salvageable and you want reconciliation at some point should not have any bearing on the need to activate the no contact rule. No contact is not always permanent. Frankly, the temporary no contact rule seems to work well with people who are open to change. Going no contact gives you an excellent opportunity to regain your peace, begin the healing process, and ultimately strengthen yourself by renewing the mind and discovering yourself.

Deploying the no contact protocol will most likely bring the controller to either a place of intense anger or rage or they may intensify their assassination of your character in demonizing you to other family members. Don't be surprised if they go to the pastor of your church and complain about your decision.

Unfortunately, many churches today do not have equipped personnel to understand the inner workings of the spirit of Jezebel and most definitely narcissistic personality traits. Do not succumb to the pressure from others that guilt you back into connecting with the controller. There cannot be any peace until the controller gets delivered. You are not responsible for the deliverance and freedom of the controller. You must focus on yourself. Remember, you are only responsible for yourself.

#4 Distance yourself

Distancing yourself is different than going no contact.

Distancing yourself from someone could be as simple as lessening the amount of contact you have with them or emotionally detaching yourself from them. When you distance yourself from them, it does not necessarily mean that you stopped communicating with them completely. It does mean that you have minimal contact points and are selective about the topics you are willing to engage in. Distancing yourself from a controller can also mean that you change your environment. Perhaps you move to a different suburb or city or maybe another state, whereby you are essentially making it more difficult for the person to have a direct line of contact with you.

Another great way to distance yourself from a toxic person is to keep yourself preoccupied with what you want to do—healthy things that develop and grow you intellectually, emotionally, and spiritually. When you begin to focus on your wants and desires, you will naturally create space and potentially detach from controlling people.

Emotionally distancing in a healthy manner starts with self-awareness. It's essential that you recognize what you feel and understand how you respond emotionally to events and how your emotions affect your behavior. Additionally, you need to manage your feelings, which means learning how to stay focused and think clearly even when you're experiencing strong emotions such as anger. Once you increase your emotional intelligence and understand yourself, you will make better decisions and motivate yourself to live a healthy life.

Distancing yourself emotionally does not mean that you have any malice towards another person. It merely means that you manage your emotions and take responsibility for your responses based on those emotions. When you recalibrate and focus on your self-development and learn to value your life, you will begin to gravitate towards your goals and dreams. By doing so, you gradually move your focus and corresponding emotions from the controlling person to that which you find valuable to do.

The method of distancing oneself from a controller is usually done gradually over time. You essentially begin to create a new normal. Distancing from a controller does not heal the controller from the wounds that bring about the control. However, it can activate some healthy self-reflection that reveals that they are pushing the people who generally love them away from them. The primary objective of distancing from the controller is to bring peace into your life. The byproduct of distancing yourself from the controller is that hopefully, it will lead the controller down the path of their journey in deliverance, healing, and wholeness.

When you distance yourself, do not give information as to where you went. The last thing you need is the controller showing up at your house or apartment stalking you. However, if they do stalk you, notify the Police of your concern.

#5 Exit strategy

If you plan to leave or exit a relationship, you must have a game plan. Controllers look to inject fear into their victims. You need to remain calm so you can strategize your exit. Remember, you have spiritual authority and have the mental, emotional, and spiritual strength to crush the enemy's plots and schemes.

Behold, I give you the authority to trample on serpents and scorpions, and over all the power of the enemy, and nothing shall by any means hurt you - Luke 10:19

Additionally, we are told in the word of God that nothing shall have dominion over you.

For sin shall not have dominion over you .... - Romans 6:14

Do not fear! Fear keeps you in a place of torment. That is precisely what the controller wants to do. Consistently remind yourself that you have authority, love, and have been given a sound, stable mind.

For God has not given us a spirit of fear, but of power and of love and of a sound mind - 2 Timothy 1:7

#6 Planning to leave

As you formulate your strategy to distance yourself, go no contact, or altogether leave the relationship, you must have a plan. Remember, controllers are banking on the fact that you will make rational decisions. Planning puts you in the driver's seat and empowers you to take back your life. The following are some practical things that you can do to prepare to leave.

- Always have enough money readily available to take a taxi or Uber to a safe location to get you away from the controller immediately.

- You should also plan to have enough money to pay for one or more nights in a hotel or motel if necessary.

- Keep a supply of gas in your car at all times. If parking in the driveway, make sure that you back into the driveway. You want to ensure that you have a quick way out of any potentially harmful situation.

- Have an extra set of keys available in a strategic area. Controllers are notorious for 'snatching' keys and FOB's to keep you from getting away.

- Make sure that you gather together essential papers such as birth certificates, Social Security numbers, vehicle license plates, titles and registrations, bank numbers, insurance papers, health records (including children's), legal documents such as loan papers, and any orders of protection papers as you may need these down the road.

- Have a "bug out bag" readily available. A bug out bag can be as big as you want it to be, but it should be something that you can grab quickly and move. You must make sure that you remain mobile at all times. The controller looks to block your positioning and movement. You need to be one step ahead of the controllers' narcissistic game plan. The primary purpose of a bug out bag is to enable you to evacuate quickly. Some items to include in your bug out bag are a change of clothing for yourself and children if necessary, a small amount of cash, prescription medications, snacks, bottled water, a phone charger, flashlight, and self-safety Instruments such as a personal alarm siren, and perhaps pepper spray. It's also recommended that you have a prepaid credit card. Controllers are notorious for canceling credit cards (financial control) to limit your options.

- Depending on how involved you were with this person, you may need to go entirely off the grid, which means that only a limited number of people need to know where you are. This may be something that you only need to do temporarily. You must be cautious in the information that you give to people. Additionally, do not tell the controller that you are going to leave. Just leave.

- It is recommended that you change your cell phone number or block the controller and their' flying monkeys' from getting their call through to you. Lastly, if you have any accounts where you shared a digital login or password, make sure that you change your passwords.

#7 Should you call the Police?

Depending on how narcissistic the controller is, there may be times where you may need to call the police. While this will usually not be the case, we need to discuss it if the situation merits it.

Decide ahead of time what circumstances will warrant you're calling the police, whether it is the next time you're threatened or if the controller violates a physical boundary and enters your property without your consent. If you're physically assaulted, then the police should be called immediately. Under no circumstances can violence be tolerated and should be reported to local authorities immediately. While you may feel as though you are betraying a loved one by calling the police, the reality is that you must protect yourself and if you have children, protect them as well. The control, threats, and abusive behavior must stop!

Keep a journal of the various details' and situations surrounding an event that might warrant a call to the police. Take pictures of any physical abuse, property damage, and any other evidence. Record the dates of the incident and any witnesses that were there when the event occurred. If you have any court documents such as a restraining order or no-contact order, ensure that you have these things available to show the police should you need to. Be aware that there probably will not be an arrest made in many situations unless there is probable cause to believe that a crime has been committed, such as an assault against or injury to you.

#8 Love and value you

"...... Love your neighbor as yourself" – Luke 10:27

Extremely critical to breaking free from the controller is to develop a love for self and have a value system in place where you are the priority in life. Does this statement shock you? If it does, it's likely because you came from a family of origin that did not teach you how to value or love yourself, or perhaps you've been indoctrinated by religious systems that in some cases teach the opposite.

Unfortunately, today many Christians and non-Christians alike suffer from a devalued core. A devalued core is common in people that continue to tolerate being controlled. Much of this comes from their insecurity, wounds, and abuse during their early childhood developmental years and teen years. One of the common symptoms of a devalued core is the insatiable need to connect with other people regardless of how healthy they are. In many cases, a person who has a devalued core will most likely attract and be attracted to emotionally unhealthy and dysfunctional people.

Love, value, and respect for self is a mindset that should have been developed as a young child from your family of origin. Practically every child needs the same thing - love, affirmation, validation, attention, protection, correction (not criticism), and training. God, our creator, places this responsibility on parents, with an emphasis on fathers.

*Fathers, do not irritate and provoke your children to anger
[do not exasperate them to resentment], but rear them [tenderly]
in the <u>training</u> and discipline and the counsel and admonition of
the Lord - Ephesians 6:4 AMPC*

*Direct your children onto the right path, and when they are
older, they will not leave it - Proverbs 22:6 NLT*

*Point your kids in the right direction — when they're old
they won't be lost - Proverbs 22:6 MSG*

However, if you did not receive these things, then there will
be some emotional growth deficiencies. You end up meandering
through life, still looking for the things you lacked when you were
younger. The danger is that you end up engaging in unproductive
behavior or entering into toxic relationships, searching for or
receiving what you did not get when you were younger. That is a
prime opportunity for a controlling person to connect with you or
for you to connect with controlling organizations.

Consider for a moment that when you were younger, you
possibly went through some type of trauma. Most of us
experienced some level of trauma when we were younger.
Experiencing trauma does not mean that you will suffer for the
rest of your life. The key is, did you get through the trauma? It
was the responsibility of your parents to get you through early
childhood trauma. For example, when you were younger, you fell
off your bicycle and scraped your knees and the palms of your
hands, possibly bleeding; if you're like most of us, you ran home
to your mom or dad or somebody in your household. Most likely,
they held you, washed your hands, washed up your knees, put a
happy face Band-Aid on your wounds, kissed you on your

forehead, and off you went – back outside on the bike. That is an example of experiencing trauma and getting through the trauma. But what, for instance, if you didn't get through that trauma? What does that do emotionally to a little child, and what effect may it have in adult life? What if the trauma is much more significant than falling off your bicycle? Perhaps the death of a parent or some other family member. Or you may have witnessed some corrupt or violent act. What about if there was inappropriate touching, molestation, or abuse? And worse yet, what if any of the trauma came from your family of origin?

Top 5 childhood traumas

- Rejection
- Incest
- Molestation
- Verbal/emotional abuse
- Physical abuse

These things and more can cause severe damage to your emotional core development, leaving you to feel unwanted, worthless, insignificant, unlovable. They can develop within you low self-esteem, a sense of inferiority, and a lack of self-confidence.

That is why many people walk around with a negative view of self and think things like:

- "I'll never be good enough"
- "I can't do it"
- "I will never measure up to others"

- "I was born on the wrong side of the tracks."
- "I am a failure at everything"

These are all debilitating views that need to be replaced by a healthier perspective of self.

#9 Stop living in the past

Your past does not define your destiny, nor does history determine your identity. We have all experienced adverse events, verbal abuse, rejection, and perhaps even physical abuse. Many have engaged in multiple relationships where they were abused and were left wounded by some controlling nuclear narcissist. Yes, we must acknowledge that we have been done wrong by people, including those we loved and those who should have loved us. It is indeed a travesty that we went through these things, and it can be challenging to let go of the experiences that have caused such great pain and suffering. However, you can control your life and leave the past behind.

You must refuse to be a victim of past things that, in most cases, you had virtually no control over. Past trauma, relationships, failures, or behaviors do not need to be a 'ball and chain' in your life any longer. It is time for you to reach your full potential in life by emancipating yourself from the enemy's insidious attacks against your mind. These lying spirits that torment your mind and emotions want to keep you at a place of victimization. You are not a victim. You are more than a conqueror.

Nay, in all these things we are more than conquerors through him that loved us - Romans 8:37

91

Some of the most incredible things you can do to strengthen your core, increase your value towards yourself, and genuinely love yourself is to see the reflection of who you are in God's word. God is your creator, and he only speaks good things about his creation. Remember, He has never made anything defective or useless. There is a purpose in all of his creation. You have an ordained purpose and are a seed sent from the Kingdom of Heaven to the earth. You are not a mistake; you are purposely formed in fashion by God for such a time as this.

For I know the thoughts that I think toward you, says the LORD, thoughts of peace and not of evil, to give you a future and a hope - Jeremiah 29:11

#10 Forgive yourself

To truly love and value yourself, you are going to need to forgive yourself. Unforgiveness and bitterness towards past things people did to you or the things you participated in or allowed will anchor you in that place of the past. There simply is no way that you can think of a bright and healthy future when you continuously see the experiences of the past. It does no good to hold onto the negative emotions, whether you did something wrong or someone hurt you.

Everyone has made mistakes in their life, and you have to forgive yourself for those mistakes. Most people have more hatred toward themselves than others. When you feel the guilt and condemnation of the past, your mind will subconsciously gravitate to doing one of two things. One of them is to try to repay or right the wrong of your mistake, often excessively. If you think that there is nothing you can do to make something right, the second option you may choose (unconsciously) is to punish yourself. There is absolutely no value in punishing oneself. So, forgive yourself and learn from your experiences in life.

#11 Self-respect

Respect yourself enough to be able to walk away from anything that no longer serves you, grows you, increases you, makes you happy, or contributes to you. Divest from relationships that do not celebrate you. Go where you're celebrated, not where you're tolerated.

A person with self-respect simply likes themself. Their self-respect is not based on successes or failures. It just IS. They respect themself because they value themselves.

When you have self-respect and accept yourself as a whole person, you will find that your relationships are very healthy. When you understand your worth and will not let anyone treat you in a controlling manner, nor will you tolerate verbal, mental, emotional, or physical abuse. You will disconnect from toxic and septic people and gather around healthier positive people.

#12 Your Internal View

Self-image is the personal view that you have of yourself. It is your internal mental picture or self-portrait of how you see yourself. Self-image is important because it affects how you relate, respond, and react in life. Your self-image is not something that is based on reality. Your self-image is primarily built based on your perception of reality or how you believe others view you. An unhealthy self-image exists when a person fixes their thoughts on their faults and shortcomings and consistently criticizes or judges their decisions, behavior, and appearance. A healthy self-image is based on the conclusion that you are a unique and valuable person and that what others or society thinks about you is unimportant.

Self-worth is an internal state of being that comes from self-love and self-acceptance. It is how you value yourself, regardless of what others think about you. It's not based on external views, but instead, it's solely based on your internal view of self. Healthy self-worth places tremendous value on who you are at your core. To know your identity, you will need to go to the source of your creation. The creative source of all humanity is God.

Then the LORD God formed the man from the dust of the ground. He breathed the breath of life into the man's nostrils, and the man became a living person - Genesis 2:7 NLT

#13 Who am I?

The failure for someone to properly identify themselves creates an open porthole into the world of controlling witchcraft spirit.

The real you is the soul man. Your body and your genetic coding came from your biological mother and father. Your soul consists of your mind, will, and emotions and came from God.

When you were conceived in your mother's womb, God supernaturally breathes the breath of life into you, and you became a living soul. That breath of God released destiny, purpose, ability, and giftings into you. Understand that your life is similar to a seed.

For example, look within the acorn seed. It is a fully formed oak tree. You may not see the oak tree in the acorn, but once the acorn is planted, it will blossom into the fully formed massive oak tree and bring forth fruit if the conditions are right.

It is imperative to understand that the circumstances, situations, trauma, or abuse that you experienced in life are things that happen to you, but they are - <u>NOT</u> you! These things are the enemy's schemes to distract you and keep you from realizing who you truly are. The enemy's goal is to devour people from ever realizing their full potential in life.

Be sober, be vigilant; because your adversary the devil, as a roaring lion, walketh about, seeking whom he may devour - 1 Peter 5:8

Once you understand who you truly are and change how you see yourself, it will not matter how other people see you or how they speak about you. Once you embrace yourself despite your mistakes, shortcomings, and limitations, you will find that your sense of value or self-worth increases. Once you understand that you are a seed and everything you need in life is within you - you can begin the journey of discovering yourself.

#14 Renew your Mind

The mind is the battlefield of your life. By far, renewing your mind is the most important thing you can do to break free from controlling people, relationships, and organizations. Actually, outside of the born-again experience, renewing the mind should be the main focus in your life. What you think and the way you think must be challenged.

For as he thinketh in his heart, so is he - Proverbs 23:7

What you think, deep within your subconscious mind (heart), is what you ultimately become. What you think affects how you feel (emotions), how you feel affects how you behave (actions), and how you behave will bring about your life results.

Thoughts ➡ Feelings ➡ Actions = <u>Results</u>

In Romans chapter 12:2 the Apostle Paul instructs the believers in Rome to:

"Be ye transformed by the renewing of your mind ..."

Renewing your mind means bringing your thoughts and imaginations into an agreement with the word of God. Therefore, whatever God thinks about you, you should think the same thoughts about yourself. When you read the word of God, you will find out that God never speaks negatively about his creation but rather expresses his delight and pleasure with us. What we see in the word of God is that, as believers, we must recognize the good in us.

..... that the participation in and sharing of your faith may produce and promote full recognition and appreciation and understanding and precise knowledge of every good [thing] that is ours in [our identification with] Christ Jesus [and unto His glory] -Philemon 1:6 AMPC

#15 Think Better - Think Positive

Summing it all up, friends, I'd say you'll do best by filling your <u>minds</u> and meditating on things true, noble, reputable,

96

authentic, compelling, gracious—the best, not the worst; the
beautiful, not the ugly; things to praise, not things to curse -
Philippians 4:8 MSG

If you want better results and relationships in life, you're going to have to think better about yourself and your entire environment. Achieving your goals in life and realizing your destiny is mostly based on what and how you think. Only you can decide what your mindset is going to be. And even though your upbringing, family of origin, and others had a tremendous impact on your thinking up to now, you can decide to take back your mind.

Now, you may be saying to yourself that you never lost your mind that you've had it the whole time. Actually, in some cases, your mind has been hijacked, and in most cases, it has been programmed. The programming that you received came early on in life. Some of it was good; some of it was not so good. And in extreme cases, it was downright horrible. Now many years removed from your early childhood developmental years, you think and act fundamentally on those (programmed) thoughts.

After years of being in dysfunctional relationships and being controlled, it's time to create the life you want by shifting your mindset and focusing on what you desire, not what you have. Stop letting the current situation direct the rest of your life. Renewing the mind is about changing from the inside outward. Do not look to the outside for change when the real issue is within. You cannot control what is out 'there'; however, you can and must control that which is within you. You either take charge of your thoughts, or you accept them from outside sources.

Controlling people cannot prevent you from creating a new mindset. People can do a lot of things to you. For example, they can take your money; they can take your car and take your rights. But what they cannot take is your mind.

To renew your mind, you must be delivered. You must begin to do something different to get the mind reconditioned to what you want. Those self-limiting beliefs and a poor view of self are lodged deep within the subconscious mind. The more you meditate on positive things and begin to use your imagination to paint the life you want; it will undoubtedly come to pass.

"Your imagination is your preview of life's coming attractions." - Albert Einstein

Your imagination is your spiritual womb. It is the place of conception for your life's journey and the place where words or imaginations are conceived and subsequently grow.

In like fashion, consider the female's womb being the place where the baby grows. It is within the womb that the baby is formed into what it is going to be. At the appointed time, the baby is born. It is within the womb that you became the physical person. In the womb, you received your physical distinctions. Now, compare this with the mind. The mind is the womb of your destiny. If you can understand that the physical womb is where we were formed, you can understand that the mind is the place where vision, ideas, and innovation is created. The mind is where we will excel or fail in getting to our destiny. It is in the mind where you become that person you think you are. When you change how you think about yourself, you will become that person that God designed to be. Your thoughts and imaginations are critical to discovering yourself

Can you imagine your life without controlling people in it? Can you imagine in your life where you are no longer abused? Can you imagine yourself realizing those dreams and visions that you thought would never manifest? It is possible – all you need to do is believe.

Jesus said unto him, If thou canst believe, all things are possible to him that believeth - Mark 9:23

And Jesus looking upon them saith, With men it is impossible, but not with God: for with God all things are possible - Mark 10:27

#16 Affirmations

Affirmations are written or spoken positive statements that, when consistently practiced, rewire our thoughts and beliefs (and therefore emotions).

Suppose you have a negative belief (or stronghold) that causes you to feel insignificant and unworthy. In that case, you can replace it with an empowering thought of significance and self-worth by repeating affirmations to yourself consistently, such as when the negative belief is triggered. If you do these at pre-determined times of the day, it will eventually become embedded into your subconscious mind. Over time these affirmations become habituated, and you become emotionally glued to them. When that happens, you believe them, and you're on your way to the NEW YOU!

Here a sample of affirmations you can use to improve your view of self. Each day, take a few minutes, stand in the mirror, and say these out loud to yourself:

- "I am a valuable person"
- "I have a healthy self-image"
- "I love myself unconditionally"
- "I accept me for who I am"
- "I matter"
- "I am confident in myself and when dealing with others"
- "I am courageous and bold, and I can be assertive while remaining humble"
- "I acknowledge every good and perfect thing that God has placed in me"
- "I am fearfully and wonderfully made in the image of God"
- "I am important"
- "My life is a gift from God"
- "I invest in me because I am valuable"
- "I attract, and I am attracted to healthy and positive people"
- "I am not ashamed of who I am"
- "I have been made in the image and likeness of God"

Another beneficial practice is to go to sleep listening to healthy and Godly "I Am" affirmations. The best time to do this is right before and during sleep. This is because your subconscious (heart) is open to receiving that which you pump into it. Do it consistently long enough and notice the results in your life.

Deliverance from controlling spirits

#17 Renounce

No More will I allow players, haters, and manipulators to control my life.

No More will Satan control me because I am delivered from his power.

No More will demons operate in and control my life.

No More will I allow the demons of fear to control my life.

No More will I allow the demons of rejection to control my life.

No More will I allow rebellion and disobedience to control my life.

No More will I open the door for demons to enter through the mind-controlling tactics of Jezebel.

No More will the demon of mind control affect my thinking; I sever all the tentacles of mind control.

No More will I allow the enemy to control my will, but I submit my will to the will of God.

No More will I allow the enemy to control my emotions, but I yield my feelings to the joy and peace of God.

No More will I allow the enemy to control my sexual character, but I yield my body as a living sacrifice.

No More will I allow the enemy to control my mind, but I renew my mind with the Word of God.

No More will I allow the enemy to control my appetite, but I yield my appetite to the control of the Holy Spirit.

No More will I allow the enemy to control my tongue, but I yield my tongue to the Holy Spirit.

No More will I allow the enemy to control any part of my life; my life is submitted to the Holy Spirit and Word of God.

No More will I allow the enemy to control my destiny, but God is the author, revealer, and finisher of my future.

#18 Prayers that break Controlling Spirits

Father, in the name of Jesus, I come to you, and I thank you for providing me with this prayer of deliverance. I ask you, God, in Jesus' name that you pull back your bow and release the arrow of deliverance into the liver of the enemy right now.

I submit to God and resist the enemy; therefore, he must flee far from me.

I exercise my authority and bind demonic principalities powers rulers of the darkness and all spiritual wickedness in high places, dominions, and Jezebelic like networks assigned to me from when I was in my mother's womb.

I break the curse of controlling spirits going back ten generations on both sides of my family bloodline. I command all witchcraft spirits, spirits that want control, mind binding spirits, schemes, plots, and snares that look to steal my purpose and destiny in life.

I command control, manipulation, intimidation, domination, lust, perversion, unforgiveness, bitterness, deception, delusion, doubt, unbelief, pride, and fear to loose me and let me go in Jesus' name.

All insecurity, low self-esteem, inferiority, rejection, fear of rejection, self-rejection, accusation, spirits of blame, shame and condemnation, disconnect from my life right now.

I command all soul ties, confederacies, associations, partnerships, and alliances to be severed. I disconnect from any emotion connected to the controller in my life.

I emancipate myself from fear, paranoia, suspicion, and phobias of all types pertaining to control manipulation, intimidation, and domination.

I believe and confess with my month that: "I do not possess a spirit of fear but rather have power, love, and a sound and stable mind."

I thank God that I am now cleansed spirit, soul, and body from all gaslighting techniques used against me. I am no longer double-minded but rather set my mind on things above rather than things beneath.

I take authority over all assassination demons. All demonic henchmen, you are commanded to cease your operations in the mighty name of Jesus, and I exercise my covenant right according to the word of God to torment you by sending you into the dry places.

I believe I have the mind of Christ, and therefore my mind is now free, my emotions are now stable and healthy, and my body is healthy.

I release the light of God into every dark place of my life to expose all the works of the enemy and every demonic seed that was planted to bring damage to my life.

I command the Mother-child relationship and the Father-child relationship to be broken.

I emancipate myself from Jezebel's web of destruction; therefore, I am free from all controlling entities.

All spirits of ugliness, self-hate, loneliness, despair, discouragement, hopelessness, suicide, death, confusion, betrayal, misery, torment, torture, guilt, shame, and condemnation to depart from my presence in the name of Jesus.

All spirits of fear of giving and receiving love freely, fear of failure, fear of success, fear of death, fear of dying loose your hold from my life and let me go!

All evil spirits of contention, biting, vandalism, corruption, child abuse, separation, bruised emotions, stress, anxiety, nervousness, I command you to cease your operations right now in Jesus' name.

I break the curse of evil memory recall and cancel its assignment against my life to self-destruct.

I break the curse of automatic failure syndrome going back ten generations on both sides of the family bloodline. All spirits of poverty, failure, self-sabotage lose your hold and let me go in Jesus' name.

Finally, I cancel out and make useless every retaliatory spirit. No weapon formed against me will prosper. I am free because I have chosen to be free. My mind is being renewed because I decide to renew my mind.

Other Books by Robert & Dixie Summers

Deliverance Training Manual - 101©

It's about Time

Genuine Fathers – Willing Sons ©

Kingdom Principles of Success, Wealth & Prosperity ©

Harboring the Spirit of Jezebel ©

Gossip – The Weapon of Mass Destruction ©

Throw Jezebel Down ©

Jezebels Whoredoms, Perversions and Witchcrafts ©

Deliverance Training Manual 201 ©

The Petrified Soul©

No More – No Mas©

Available at summersministries.com or on Amazon

For Professional Freedom & Transformation Coaching
please call (877) 985-1744 or visit www.icanadvance.com

Made in the USA
Middletown, DE
08 June 2023